An Interview with Kenneth Waltz

The following includes an interview with Professor Waltz conducted in August 2007 in his summerhouse in Maine and winter 2007 in New York. We were first talking about his personal history, then tackled his theoretical assumptions and the histories of his seminal books in order to finally discuss current world affairs in general.

So what I would start with are the circumstances of your childhood. Such as where were you born, where did you grow up? And when was that?
Ann Arbor, Michigan. I was born in 1924 and I lived in Ann Arbor for the next 18 years, until 1942 when I went to college at Oberlin.

Lets stay with you childhood. What did your parents do?
My father was a carpenter, painter, was a working man. When I was young, in the 1920ies, he was a pasteurizer. He was pasteurizing milk. He was head of the pasteurizing department in the Ann Arbor Dairy, but of course he was the only one in the pasteurizing department. So it was very nice. I walked down to the Ann Arbor Dairy which was a mile or so away and had lunch with him sometimes and then of course I would get all the ice-cream I could eat because that was the Dairy that made ice-cream and everything else.

What was the relation to your father like?
Oh, I liked my father. He was very relaxed and as I grew older I thought all too willing to take orders from my mother.

What did your mother do?
You know, in those days being a mother and house-wife was considered a full time job. We had a big garden, she did a lot of canning and making of jellies, she canned a lot of tomatoes and string beans, all those things. We had a place in the basement, you know, the cool part of the basement, it was walled off. And we had stacks of these things which we could eat all during the winter. There was a root seller, he had carrots and cabbages and potatoes and all that during the winter. I am sure it was the same in Germany.

Can you describe your relationship to your parents? Can you give examples?
I think my mother was very good when I was young, when I was little, teaching me to read before I went to school, and when I had quite a bit of trouble with my legs, my one leg, because

it was broken and never set. So, it did not grow back together very well. And she would sometimes – so I could go to school – she would pull me on the sled to the school, which was probably 3/8th of a mile from my house. And then she'd come and pull me back, uphill. And looking back on it, that was very good of her. She really did care and then I would get an education, which of course she did not have, nor did my father.

And the relation to your father, something typical?
I would say typical of that era, I mean he was just – you could ask my wife – he was just a nice person, very hard working. And of course during the depression it was very difficult. I can remember when he because of stomach trouble had to give up being a pasteurizer and he was making 15 dollars a week working in a hotel. Even during the depression 15 dollars a week was bad. 15 dollars plus meal. On Sunday after church he would have Sunday lunch with us and he never ate much because he felt guilty. He could have been eating at the hotel instead of eating family food. He was a very nice person.

Did you have siblings?
Oh no, I am an only child.

Did you parents were idols for you in any respects?
Oh yeah, I admired my father. He was such a hard worker and steadfast. He was not an intellectual, far from it.

The most happy or worst experience in childhood?
I enjoyed my childhood. You know, I am sure there were bad moments, but they don't stand out in my mind. I can't think of any that I would call worst moment, or best moment. Nothing comes to mind.

Did they encourage you to go to university?
Oh yeah, oh sure. They wanted me to go to college. Oh yes.

So you indicated that both parents supported your education.
Well, not financially then. But they were in favour of my going to the … well everybody in Ann Arbor of course assumed that one would go to the University of Michigan. I assumed that. But luckily, I was friends with two people – Eric and Maria Walter – their father was then associate Dean at the University of Michigan. And he pointed out to his kids that they don't have to go to

the University of Michigan, there are other places. And he mentioned Oberlin College, which you may never have heard of. And I remember Eric and I went into the principal's office and said: Why are students here never informed about opportunities for scholarships and places other than the University of Michigan? And the high school principal said: Well, everybody goes to the University of Michigan, there is no point telling people. Well, by that time I was not getting along at all well with my mother and I wanted to go somewhere other than … if I wanted to go to the University of Michigan, I would have to live at home, because of lack of money. So, Dean Walter and his wife drove his son and his daughter and me to Oberlin and we took scholarship exams. And I took the exam in Mathematics and in short order I got an offer for one semester scholarship, tuition. And then just a couple of days later I got a letter of the University of Michigan saying: 4 years scholarship. So, I wrote to Oberlin and said: Much though I would like to come to Oberlin, and I meant it, I can't because you know four years against one! I got a letter back saying: Well and behold, just as we received your letter we were considering you for a full tuition 4 years scholarship. I did not know I was bargaining, but that is the best way to bargain, you know, you are doing it. It never occurred to me that one could bargain. So, I got this 4 year full tuition scholarship and I accepted it. And all three of us went, the Deans daughter and the Deans son and I.

Where did you know the Deans daughter and sons?
In high school, they were the same grade that I was in and we were friends.

How was high school time for you?
Oh high school was … In fact, I enjoyed the whole schooling in Ann Arbor. Public schooling, that was good. Let's just skip over kindergarten and all that. And in the high school … high school was so highly regarded that if one had C+ average and you were on the college curriculum, one was automatically admitted to the University of Michigan. I did not know that. I did not know that until it was almost time for me to graduate. But I had a friend who was always checking his grades. And I said: Why are you always checking your grades? He said: Well if you have a C+ average you go to the University of Michigan. So, if he had a B- average he'd work less, and if it went down to a C he'd work a little harder. So he got down to a C+ average, automatically in the University of Michigan.

What was your style of working? Did you never think about the grades?
I never thought about the grades. You know, I would not know how to get a C+. Mathematics was what I did, what I was mainly, mainly interested in. And of course you got A's.

So even in school you did mathematics?
I almost completed a mathematics major at Oberlin, I lacked one half of one course.

What about your social life at high school?
Well, it was an interesting social life. Some of the people I knew then still talk about it. I was from the Westside, now glamorized as the old Westside, which was German. There were two sides of Ann Arbor both rather highly Germanic. There was the Westside which was mainly peasant stock, I mean, farmers who had moved to the city. My mother for example ran away from her home at the age of sixteen. She had it well planned. She rode in from Saline, which is eight miles to Ann Arbor on a load of potatoes and a friend of hers, a girlfriend of hers, had arranged a job as a maid for a German family on the Eastside. The Eastside was the University of Michigan, University of Michigan hospital, which was considered to be the finest hospital in the United States. And we had the May festival, which is German, like Cincinnati. On the Eastside we had intellectuals, more affluent Germans, on the Westside you had the poorer Germans. When my wife and I went back to my high school reunions, even when she knew that Ann Arbor was German, German, German, she was still surprised: all the kids had German names. And all the parents spoke bad German and bad English, if you are on the Westside. On the Eastside it is different.

Your family has German background too?
Yeah, well. You have to understand American history. All of my parents and my grandparents and probably their parents were born in the United States. But they grew up in farming communities and they spoke German, they did not speak English. We used to go – as kids – we used to go to the 'Schwaben Verein' on Sundays, out in the woods. They would have a little dance floor and an 'Umpa' band and the beer was a nickel of a buck. And they did not mind if kids bought a mug of beer, you know. We would buy a mug of beer and later some of the older people would get a little drunk and it was a lot of fun for us. And they danced.

Did you have friends at school?
I had lots of friends at school, all way long, from kindergarten downward. Let's see. On the Westside there was only one great school and there was only one junior high school. We all started kindergarten together we grew up together and there was only then one public high school, there was the catholic high school, and there was the University high school, but the best of the three was the public school. And one of my teachers at Ann Arbor high school completed

his PhD in spring and at fall he joined the faculty of Northwestern University. It was that most of them had gone to the University of Michigan. It was an excellent education.

What was your outlook at life back then? Did you have dreams?
Well, you know, somehow, I don't know. You don't really think about these things in a very systematic, rational way. But I did know that I wanted to go to college. And I did know that my parents would not have got a lot of money to help me along. So I worked, I had a lot of jobs.

What did you do?
Well, I sold in a post office starting when I was twelve years old. Then, I worked up from there. I had two paper routes, a total of eight miles and I knew damned well to ride my bicycle. So, after school I would deliver the newspapers. I also had a separate job of collecting money from people who didn't pay, and I got five percent for all the money I collected and I singled out people with big bills, because five percent of a dollar is a nickel so you want to find somebody who owes eight dollars. Forty cents I'd get there. I repaired typewriters. I was a 'soda jerk' on and off, you know that term. That means you worked in an ice-cream place, ice-cream, sodas and sundaes, and in this case hamburgers and hotdogs and all that. 25 cents an hour, but I put in a lot of hours. I had a dispensation, I did not have to come to school at eight o'clock, the way everybody else did. I could come at nine. Because I had this job and I worked sometimes until two o'clock in the morning. And I started driving a truck, which was illegal, I wasn't old enough to get a licence to drive a truck, I had a licence to drive a car. But I drove a delivery truck. I used to go down to the Michigan central railway and pick up the New York Times, it usually came about one o'clock at Sunday morning. And then, I would deliver them to various drugstores and news stores in Ann Arbor

You had many jobs, but did you have also hobbies?
Well, I always wanted to play the piano, but I didn't have a piano. So, I played the Banjo. When I was beginning to make enough money, you know I was really saving it, but when I was sixteen I bought a piano and took piano lessons.

You can play piano?
Well, the trouble is when you are sixteen, and you got a lot of other things to do, beginning to start off very seriously ... though I did a lot of practicing. And then you become seventeen and there are girls, and you know, and then more and more jobs, because, from 1940 onwards, really 1940, I joined the surveyors crew, the Ford bomber plant was being built outside of Ypsilanti,

which is near Ann Arbor and that meant the need for low cost housing. So, land had to be surveyed and so I got a job with the surveying crew. In fact, in my last year of high school I did not really go to high school much. I was just too busy making money and the money was getting better and better because of the war. Even before we were in the war the employment began to get better. But yeah, I always had a lot of friends and high school dances and high school romances and all of that.

So you were very active.
I was the class orator. We had things like that.

What does the orator do?
The orator orates. In other words, at the graduation you give an oration. You know you have to work on that, you are standing up there, in front of the graduation. This was a big thing then. In small towns they still are. I mean, all the parents come and they are very proud of their kids who are probably C- students but they are getting a high school degree and all that and you stand up there and give this oration. All the parents and some other siblings who are going to graduate in the future are there. Also, I appeared in a couple of plays, starting in junior high school. I look back on it. I was the scrooge in the Christmas Carol. Why was I scrooge in the Christmas Carol? Not because I had any acting ability! It was because I was capable of memorizing the lines and standing on a stage and look at the audience and saying them out loud. But it made me think that, hey, maybe I'm going to be an actor!

Did you ever want to become anything like that?
Yeah, I thought that, hey, being an actor that'd be great. And I was in various plays thereafter. Even in my first year in college, and then I began to realize I was a lousy actor.

Were you an outstanding pupil?
Well, yeah, I was, yes.

Were you distinguishable from the other ones?
Well, yeah, I was first among the boys in the graduation class. Girls do not count because they always do homework.

Why would you say that was?

I was very good in Mathematics and mathematics takes no time. I was too in college. I mean if you are in history or English literature, what not, you are spending a little time to read this stuff. In mathematics, you either get it or you don't. If you get it – boom – you're done. And I liked, I enjoyed the mathematics. I gave it up when I was ... it was after World War II. The last mathematics course I took, I think, was in the summer at the University of Michigan. I took the graduate course in Mathematics. And then, I think, I took one more at Oberlin. And by that time I realized that I'm not going to be a first rate Mathematician, I am not going to rival other mathematicians, I should find something else to do. But I'm not sure I did the right thing. But I don't regret it, dropping it. And I thought: well ok, I am going to be a mathematical economist. I majored in economics and mathematics. Economics in those days was very badly taught and even though I did graduate in economics I kind of lost interest.

Was this decision difficult to you?

It was not so much leaving mathematics, it was thinking of something else to do.

They encouraged you to study.

They expected me to study. See, both of my parents grew up on farms outside of Ann Arbor and they probably spoke German until they went to high school. My mother went to high school, my father never went to high school. My mother had an unfortunate stepmother, and I believe that because aunts and uncles confirmed that this was an unfortunate stepmother. The real mother died. So my mother left home at the age of sixteen and became a maid. And my father, who grew up on a farm, a petty farm, land to the one side was pretty good and the other side was pretty bad, he grew up on one of those farms. The land was not very productive, and he found his way into the city. And he was a young man and he worked as a carpenter building houses and barns and he was part of a crew. He was a carpenter and a painter and as I said he got a job at the Ann Arbor Dairy as a pasteurizer. And this is back in the days when the milk was delivered in a horse cart. I can well remember that, looking back, it was romantic. But at the time, it was just the way it was. The ice wagons used to come around, horse drawn of course, in the hot summers in Ann Arbor. They gave the little kids some ice, big thrill, but probably unsanitary, but never you got sick. But, you know, the principle is hard work. My mother worked hard, my father worked hard. I worked hard myself.

What was the influence of teachers, friends? Did someone introduce you to social sciences?

I don't know what age you are thinking of. But when I was in high school, when you are asked what you want to be as a little kid, you could say: Well, I want to be a cowboy – it's an American thing - or a fireman. Then you began to realize you can't say that, when you get to be twelve years old or something like so. Then you start saying: I'm going to be an engineer. And I began to think: yeah, well, I'm going to be an engineer, this has something to do with mathematics and all that. And then when I got a bit older, say tenth, eleventh grade, I realized I don't want to be an engineer. So, then the question was: What are you going to be? And then, at the University of Michigan, there was this psychological service and you could go there for career counselling. So, when I was at junior high school I did that. It took two days, about 12 hours. And when the two days were over and I went back for the evaluation this very nice woman - I realized in retrospect that she was probably a graduate student or a young instructors wife - and she came out all smiles and she said: Your best vocational choice is to be a musician, what instrument do you play? And I said: Well, I play the banjo. And she said: Well, your second best: law. So, I said, ok. I called the dean of law school at the University of Michigan. His name was Dean Love. It tells you a lot about what the world was like then as compared to now. I called Dean Love's office. Who answered the phone? Dean Love. And I said: I'm going to college at Oberlin, but I want to come back to the University of Michigan law school and could you advise me in what best to major in. And he said: Well I can't give you that advice, but I can tell you that recently we did a survey of our graduates and the ones who were most successful majored in mathematics. And the second: English. And after that there is no good correlation. And I said, well, Mathematics. It all coincided with my interests, so I took mathematics.

When did you first detect your interest in mathematics?

Well it was just always very easy for me to do the mathematics, whatever grade you were in. You did the geometry, did the algebra, you did the trigonometry. It is fun, and begins to become creative when there is no obvious way to do it. You got to figure it out. As I said, I stuck with it, but then I realized I am not going to be a mathematical whiz, let's try something else.

Have your parents tried to influence you in this?

You know, on matters relating to higher education my parents were somewhat illiterate. Their two languages are English and German. They were, you know, they did not know anything about mathematics. They did not know what a history major might mean, or a biology major or physics major. They did not have any way of understanding those things, naturally not.

8

When did you start to study mathematics?
Actually, I did not really decide to do that. It is just when you were in college preparatory curriculum in Ann Arbor you took mathematics every year. I guess you did not have to, I guess you probably had only to have to take it two years instead of four years. But see, a lot of people and most of my friends did and all the girls did. It's just what you did. And think you had to take one year of science but you could take two. So, I took physics, which I liked. And I took chemistry, which I thought was kind of boring. Chemistry was boring in those days. Biology was boring. Biology is very exciting now, but not in those days. Who was the scientist who said: there is physics and there is 'stamp collecting'. Meaning: biology, chemistry, those are all stamp collecting. There is one science: physics. I did not think this was true when I was a kid. But I liked physics, I liked mathematics, and I did not like chemistry. And I never took biology, but I was never tempted to take it.

Did you think about becoming a scholar back then?
No, no, I used to firmly believe that there were two things I did not want to do. I did not want to teach and I did not want to write. I believed it. That was one reason I shifted from mathematics to economics. I thought: well, in economics you can go into business, you can go into government you don't have to be a teacher or writer. There are a lot of other things you can do. You know, these are not decisions you make. This is just the way your life develops.

What is it that you did not like about teaching or writing?
Oh, I like it know. But then I thought: I don't want to teach or write, because I did not know. I had never taught.

How did your studies progress from an undergraduate at Oberlin onwards?
By and large economics was badly taught and I found it to be fairly boring. But I stuck with it because, as I said before, I could go into business or government or what not. In other words, it was avoiding a decision rather than making one. And I completed the major. And then, of course, I was realizing along about my junior year that I did not really want to be a lawyer. It is really convenient if you have something you can say. Well, what do you want to be? Well, I want to be a lawyer. It does not mean you really want to be a lawyer. It means just that. It may mean that. But it may also mean that you are avoiding making a decision. So, you got something to say: Well, I am going to be a lawyer. And then I said: Oh my god, I don't want to study law. It's what seemed to be the most boring thing that one could do. So, again, I fell back on economics. Again, I did, technically, I did a year of graduate work in economics and in fact what I did was the first

semester of economics and in the second semester I realized I did not really want to do economics. So, I thought, well, what are the things you enjoyed most? And the answers were quite easy. One was literature. And the other was political - we call it political theory, really political philosophy, it's not theory. You know, Plato, Locke, Hobbes, all that. Which I loved, I still do. So, the second semester of my graduate work in economics, I did not do any economics. All I did was a lot of literature courses at Columbia. The literature department was excellent, so I had some really great courses. And I had political philosophy, which was a little slim at Columbia then. But then comes the time you have got to make a decision. And by this time I met my wife, and she suffered through this with me. You know: What am I going to be, what I am going to do? And well, if I'd do English literature, I am not going to write a poem and I am not going to write a novel, I am going be a critic. This, I think, is a perfectly honourable thing to be. But just being a critic did not really inspire me. So, I thought: aha, political philosophy. And in fact, my wife and I went back to Oberlin, we were on the way to Ann Arbor to visit my parents, and we stopped in Oberlin and I talked to two people who really inspired me: John Lewis and his wife, both of whom were theorists. And I said: Well, I am thinking about becoming a college teacher in political philosophy. And they both said: Well, it's a wonderful life if you have some money. College pay then was really pretty poor. So, we decided to do that. My wife and I both did graduate work at Columbia together and both in political theory.

How old were you when you went from Oberlin to Columbia?
You see, I'd been in World War II, so I went to Columbia January or February 1948.

So you have been to WWII, can you tell me about this?
I was on that boat, going to … you know, you did not know where you are going, but in retrospect we were going to the Philippine islands, specifically to Manila. And while we were on the boat, this was July or August 1945, a rumour spread around the boat. There was no announcement, but a rumour spread around the boat that some unusual kind of bomb had been dropped on Japan. It was just a rumour. And of course that was - I know now - August 6th, 1945; that was the atomic bomb. We were, again in retrospect, we were to be the second wave. We were going over as replacements, and I thank god for the atomic bomb as Paul Fussell … you know probably his piece, its … I assigned it, as a matter of fact, its worth reading. There are still people who think we should not have dropped it. I will thank god for the atomic bomb and I am with him on it. He has not been in the second wave, but it does not make any difference what wave you are in. Or what branch you are. I had been in the quarter masters, but I mean …. At the beaches of Han Shu, the gun emplacements were very impressive. They would blast you out

of the water. The guns were not there, but the emplacements were there. The chances were very high that I would have been dead. But the atomic bomb saved us and saved them. The casualties on both sides would have been horrendous. I spent a year there and then went back to Oberlin.

What did you learn from the war?
I think nothing beyond the obvious. War is terrible. If you are in the army or any branch of service, and you think: Jesus, when it comes to it, I am going to shoot somebody, to kill him. And most normal people don't want to do that. And of course the military is very good, as they have to be, about indoctrination. I mean, that is true of all the militaries of all the nations in the world. I mean, you have to get these by and large young people to think that, boy, those adversaries are evil. And you've got to kill them. But then the thought of it! And the American army, as you probably know, is different - at least was different - from other armies. You shot at people. Most armies in those days just shot, just to mow them down. But the American army, because of the frontier and all that, you were taught to aim at individuals. And the idea of - you know, you don't know this guy - the idea of aiming at somebody to try to kill him, and you know you have got to do it because, if you don't kill him he is going to kill you, or maybe. So, I mean, you know, I don't like that.

Was there any specific experience in the war that you still clearly remember?
I kind of hate to say it, but there is the English meaning of "he had a good war". You know what that means in the English context. And then there is the other meaning of "he had a good war". I had a good war in that other meaning. Nobody shot at me. I did not shoot at anybody. I met some interesting people, a couple of whom are still good friends of mine and now my wife's. I did have a couple of very interesting experiences. I spent probably two million dollars in 1945 money, which is like 20 million dollars now, before I was old enough to sign contracts. I bought coal for the night service command, which is West coast. It was my job. I mean, I went to the army, I spent four months in basic and advanced training and then I went to the officers' candidate's school and became a second lieutenant. And then I was shipped to Seattle, and by accident I became a buyer of coal. We bought - and there were two of us - we bought 125 thousand tons of coal for one camp, Fort Lewis and Fort Washington. We bought a lot of coal. And as I said, I was not even old enough to sign my contracts, only 20 years old. Someone else had to sign my contracts. That was quite an experience for a young fellow.

Let's get back to your studies. When and why did you decide to go to Columbia, did you have an offer?
Yeah, I definitely had an offer, I had the GI bill! You know, if you were a veteran of World War II, you could go to any authorized educational enterprise. It did not have to be a college or university, could be a vocational thing. You could go to Heidelberg; you could go to the University of Paris. And your tuition would be paid, and a stipend and books. So, I don't even remember any of my friends who were veterans even thinking about scholarships or fellowships. You did't need them. And this made a big difference in American life, I mean, higher education just exploded because you had all these guys like me who could go to any university they wanted to go to and be paid for it.

So, why the decision for Columbia?
You know what is surprising even now: an awful lot of kids who go to graduate school don't know, they don't really pick graduate schools because of certain professors. They pick graduate schools because of "Oh Harvard, Harvard that must be great!". Things like that. That non-reasoning kind of "I don't know anything but I heard that Harvard must be great". Well, in Ann Arbor high school there was something called the Washington club trip which met about four, five days in Washington and several days in New York City and boy I just ... I fell in love with New York City. I just thought New York City was wonderful. I like Washington too, but New York City was exciting. So, yeah, Columbia, Jesus, I could go to Columbia. And then it turned out the economic department was terrible. But it was New York City.

Can you tell me about your first years at Columbia?
Well, I told you one semester of economics was more than enough. I told you about the second semester. And then I went through another crisis such as in high school: what the hell am I going to do. And I decided with my wife that political philosophy was it. I had to go to some people in economics faculty. I had to get them to write letters to say: Please take this student - it was called the Public Law and Government Department - into the Public Law and Government Department, which I then did. And my wife and I would get together and we both really enjoyed the political theory stuff. Now, at Columbia in those days we had hordes of graduate students because of the GI bill. Most of them were not at all qualified. Rumours were that the system was very funny. You did not have to take any course for credit except for a one-year seminar. The rules were changed shortly thereafter. But that is all I had to do is take a one-year seminar for credit. Other than that you had to have courses, but you didn't have to have grades.

You were free to choose?

So, right, it was like the European system. Nobody knew you, nobody knew if you were attending classes or not attending classes, except of the one seminar. So, most people did as I did. They would take some courses for credit because they liked the course. And because they needed something on their record, some grades. And then, all you had to do to get a master's degree was a low hurdle exam. I never heard of anybody flunking, it was nothing. And then, to be admitted to the PhD programme, a two-hour oral. No written. A two-hour oral, and the rumour was that two thirds of the people flunked, I think it was probably only three fifths, still high. But all of the students believed two thirds. An awful lot of students just never took the orals, they just gave up. They said: I can't do it, I can't, I can't face it. Well, I took the orals and I enjoyed them. It was fun. And then my major was political theory and my minor was international relations. And the pressure I was under was this: my wife was pregnant and I faced fatherhood and these crucial oral exams and the army, which had recalled me for the Korean war. So, I spent that year preceding the orals, fighting off the army, asking for stays of exemption, so to speak, postponing, so I could take the orals and so I could be there for the birth of the baby. It was a fretful year. You know, ordinarily you could put the orals off, but you just postpone it for a semester or whatever, but knowing I was going to have to go to Korea, I mean that is … I mean you lose a lot, you are going to be out of it, out of the academic action for two years, and it's not like starting over. So, I felt that I had to do three things: postpone the army, do the orals and be around for the birth of the baby. I was actually in the army by the time the baby was born but I was able to be there. And the key person in my minor, which was International Relations, was Bill Fox. I don't know if you have ever heard of him. William T. R. Fox, often called 'superpower Fox' because he wrote that superpowers book. And he was impressed. And before I went to Korea I was in Virginia, I wrote a proposal for a PhD dissertation, which was based on an idea which I had developed when reading for the exams in IR. This was an experience because the person who was to be the principal examiner in IR customarily made agreements with people who were merely minors. You know, you covered certain things and not others. My agreement was that I'd do imperialism, I would do European diplomatic history, foreign policy, but I would not do international law, I would not do international organization. And then he got sick. And Bill Fox, from whom I had never taken a course, was filling in for this other guy, Ned Peffer. So, I was saying: Well, I have this agreement with Professor Peffer, and I explained it. And he said: I have never heard of any such agreements. So, he called the secretary of the department who knew everything and she said: Yes, Professor Peffer did that, he made agreements with minor students of this sort. Well Bill hung up. I did not call him Bill then of course. He swung his chair around and said: Nevertheless, if you are going to do IR, you are going to do IR, you are not

13

going to do pieces of it! And I said: But I finished my preparation, I only have three weeks left, and then I am going to go to the army! I finished my preparation in International Relations. I want to spend the rest of my time on my major! He said: If you are going to do IR, you are going to do IR. Boy, my wife and I got busy. We went to the library looking for power, power, because it was superpower Fox. All that. And in the course of doing all this reading that was when I thought of "Man, the State and War". That's when I figured out what was wrong with the field. That the people writing in International Politics, all smart guys, were writing from three basic different assumptions. So that became my dissertation. So, Bill Fox was right, if you are going to do IR, you do IR. And then for years thereafter I was always convinced ... I think that "Man, the State and War" meant that everybody thought of me as being in international politics, and I thought political philosophy! So, I was always looking for that chance to get back into the political philosophy business. And in fact the last time I taught, that was "Plato to Locke", the last time I taught it that was at Brandeis in probably 1965, and that cured me. I lost my desire to do it.

You finished your studies, did your oral exams, submitted your proposal and went to Korea?
Well, I was in Korea for nine months. I was in the army for about a year and a half. I got out a bit early. I think it was supposed to be two years. It was about a year and a half.

So, you came back and wrote your PhD.
I came back in the fall of 1952 and thanks again to Bill Fox - because by that time we had the baby - he hired me as a research assistant, which paid me the same salary as if I had been an instructor. We still had instructors in those days, we don't have them anymore. Most universities don't, they are called assistant professors. It was a set salary, 3.600 dollars. There was no bargaining, I mean that was what everybody got. So I had that. And the deal was that I did half time working on my dissertation and half time working on a gargantuan manuscript by Alfred Vagts. Is that a name in Germany? He is supposed to be a German. And he wrote this mammoth. I am not exaggerating, it was that high (shows about 40 centimetres) and it was Germanic! The prose was impenetrable. It was in English. And I turned it into a book, which even went in second printing and probably a third printing. I did that half time and my dissertation half time. And in 14 months I had my dissertation done.

In 14 months?

Yeah. Well you see, it helps to have a wife and a baby. You know, you have got to make a living. The kids now of course have four years, stipends and all that, so they don't ... it's the spur of necessity.

Can I ask you about your wife? How did you meet her?

We both went to Oberlin College. We were only at Oberlin College together for one semester because of World War II for me. And I did some work at the University of Michigan, I did some work at the University of Texas, and I did some work in the American University in Washington. So, I wasn't in Oberlin all that much. So, we had that one semester and we did not know each other. And in New York City I was at Columbia she was at the treasury's department at AT&T saving up money because she wanted to do two things: go to graduate school and go to Europe. And as a result of her being at Oberlin, one Sunday afternoon an Oberlin friend of mine who had a car in New York City - it was feasible then, it is not feasible now - he said: there are four Oberlin girls, living in lower East Side, let's go and visit them. Well, I said: sure, fine. And one of them was my wife. Well, I was attracted. So, in short order we got together, that was the spring of 1948. And in June 1949 we got married. And she worked that summer, and then we enrolled at Columbia for graduate studies together.

And after the baby, what did she do?

She worked at AT&T until - what is the timing of this? - oh, she worked at AT&T through the summer of 1949 and then she became a graduate student. Then I got a called back and we went to Petersburg, Virginia, where she finished her masters essay and then I went off to Korea and she and the baby went back to Morristown, New Jersey, and stayed in her parents apartment until I came back in the fall of 1952. And then we moved to New York City, she had a part time job in Greenwich Village, she had a part time job working for a real estate agent. And you know I'd be home with the kid and she'd be - that was just one village, there was not East and West, there was the village - she would walk off to work, and I'd take care of the kid. And then she'd come back. We just had one bedroom and for the kid, living with unfolding bed and a little kitchen which was part of the living room, and it was the kind of thing you'd find hard to tolerate when you get older but when you are young it is wonderful. So, she did that and then I would take the IRT. West Village is good because you take the IRT and shot right up to Columbia; on the express subway it didn't take long. It was very nice. So, I would go to the institute to work for Bill Fox, work on the dissertation and work on Alfred Vagts.

How did Professor Fox choose you or did you choose him?
As I said, when I was, because of him, required to think of International Relations as a whole field instead of pieces, I had this idea about how to explain, or that at least people were talking past one another. It was not simply that they disagreed, that was part of it, but it was that they were just thinking in different terms or different ways. So, once I got the idea, it was applying political theory, but applying it to IR. And there was the key person in political philosophy that was Franz Neumann. And my wife and I both admired him greatly and we went to every lecture that he gave and he was extremely good. But I had this idea. So, naturally I could not do that for Franz Neumann, he did not care about International Relations. Obviously he cared about it. After all, as a German-Jewish refugee obviously he cared about it, but not as an academic discipline. So, Bill Fox was the guy I dealt with. So, I submitted a proposal and went off to Korea. I worked the proposal up when I was at Fort Lee in Virginia, and sent it to him before I went to Korea. And a couple of months after, when I was in Korea I got this letter from him - in those days all of the tenured members of the department passed on proposals for dissertations, that was a different era, inconceivable now. So, they'd have these luncheon meetings, and proposals - and Bill Foxe's letter which I remember still very well: Nobody understands what it is you proposed to do, but everybody agrees that you should be allowed to go ahead and do it.

So, the potential was already understood? Did you get support for you PhD?
Yeah, I worked for the institute. And I did get this 3.600 Dollars a year to support the family and worked half time. And I really did work about half time on Vagts and half time on my dissertation.

And what kind of effect did the book have on you and on the community?
The thinking produced the book. One of the effects of the book on me of course was that people thought of me as being international politics and I was being political theory. What effect it did have on the community? It began to acquire reputation, it began to be read more widely, it began to be used, it became more and more common to have people assign it to their classes, and first it was mainly at the graduate level and I can remember one meeting in the American Political Science Association when somebody said that he was assigning the book to his undergraduates. And this silly guy said: undergraduates? I only assign it to my graduate students! Now of course it is very much undergraduates and all the graduates students in International Relations, by the time they become graduate students it is only old heat stuff to them. I mean that it was what they read in their undergraduates. So, its influence spread.

Were you surprised by the success of the book?
Well, I did not think it would be as successful as it has been. And my wife said: Nobody is going to want to read this book because everybody knows all this! And that's of course because she had lived with it so long. It did not take me long to write the dissertation, but it took me quite some time to turn it into a book. And I am glad it did because it made it better.

How long was the dissertation?
In typescript it was 300 pages. It was not a Germanic dissertation. I mean, if you write 800 pages how can anybody say this is not a dissertation. No, this was not it.

How did you cope with the stress of having a family, having a job at this time?
You know when you are young, you can do these things. I was still fairly young. I was born in 1924, I was thirty when the dissertation was done. But I would have been younger if there had not been two wars.

When was the decision made to remain in academia?
Oh, by that time ... we made that decision when I shifted from economics to political science.

Did you ever expect that you would have such a success overall?
No, we always thought, my wife and I thought: Well, we will end up in a small college, have a nice life. Not at Oberlin, but in a place somewhere close to Oberlin. And in fact then we left Columbia. Regretfully, because by then we were about to have our third child, and we were living on an academic salary and we could not afford to send the kids to private schools. And the public schools in New York City were not satisfactory. So, we felt that we had to leave, and we, you know, were very devoted to Columbia and to New York City. Still, obviously. But we went to Swarthmore, which is a - I don't know if you know Swarthmore, but many people, including me would say, it's ... it may be the best college in the country, it is certainly among the best colleges. If you think of the best colleges you think of Amherst and Williams and not Harvard, but Swarthmore. I think, they still may be the best.

When did you go to Swarthmore?
We left Columbia 1957, went to Swarthmore and stayed there till 1966. I went there as an associate professor and left as a professor.

How did your career go on from then onwards? Did you prepare to have this success? Or did you just lead a normal life?

Yeah! I did not think of myself as a star. I mean, I was becoming better known, obviously, but I was not overwhelmed by offers from major institutions. So, you know, I had spent a year plus at Harvard, and I had spent more than a year in London. I was unattached, not with any university or institute. But in fact I got to know the people at LSE, our two favourite universities: the LSE and Columbia. And we became very fond of the London School of Economics. And still, most of the men from those days are dead, but we still are in contact. When we go to London we still see a couple of the wives of those men. Hedley Bull's, and Martin Wight's, and somebody you probably don't know: C.A.W. Manning's. C.A.W. Manning put the whole thing together. You know there are those people who have those shaping roles but they are not themselves so well known. He put the thing together. Hedley Bull and Martin Wight were two of the outstanding people. We spent 1959 and 1960 in London. And as I say, I was not at the LSE but obviously I spent some time at the LSE. We got to know these people. There is the International Relations department separate from the Politics Department, and because I was working at the second book, which was not International Relations I got to know people both at International Relations and the Politics Department, Ken Minogue for example. Other people would be a name, some of them been dead too long. But anyway I got to know both of the Politics people and the IR people very well and still every time we go to London we have lunch with Mary Bull, she lives in Oxford. She comes in and we have lunch at the Tate, which has a good dining room. Not the new Tate, the old Tate! Tate Britain. And Martin Wight's wife, they'd live outside of London, Surrey someplace. Not the last time, but the time before that, we had supper with her and Mary at the Royal Institute of International Affairs. We lived for about a total of four years in London, we feel at home there, we love it. And that's all. It's all rooted in 1959/1960.

When did the idea to Theory of International Politics come about?

Well, the next book I did was "Foreign Policy and Democratic Politics", which was quite different. And after "Man, the State and War" became somewhat known, one person, George Lawney, said to me: What will be the sequel? I said: I don't have any sequel. I don't have any idea about how to develop this further! But after the Foreign Policy and Democratic Politics, which I enjoyed doing very much, and so did my wife – it's her favourite, she likes it better than the other books - I began to think of international politics again and I was on the National Science Foundation committee. I was on the original advisory committee, there had not been one until that day and I was asked to join the committee. It was fixed term, I forgot how long it was, and because we were the first committee there would be no continuity. So, I was asked to stay on for an extra year. And I began to think about, you know, how to do theories. Most people when they say theory don't have any idea what the word means. I mean you can ... in the various usages, for example: literary theory. Hasn't anything to do with theory. Or, when lawyers talk about the theory of the case, that just means a guess about who did the crime with some evidence to back it up. It has nothing to do with theory. And certainly most people in Political Science and International Politics say: "theory ... what is it"? They say: "Well, it's not history or current events. If it is not history, it must be theory!" And I did not think that was ... I did not like that. So, I began to read a lot of philosophy of science. And the trouble with that literature is that so much of it is so good it is hard to stop reading it. But also a characteristic of the philosophers of science is that they are not any good on theories. It's about testing theory. Way down: What's a theory? They don't think about that. So, I got interested in that. And I wrote a proposal to the National Science Foundation, and they gave me a grant. A rather, I thought, rather generous grant. And I put some other grants together and spent a year in the Philosophy Department at the London School of Economics. And the Philosophy Department at the LSE is not a Philosophy Department, it's a Philosophy of Science Department. And in fact, you know, they don't teach Plato and Hegel and that. They teach Kant, which is proper. Right? Because he is really the forerunner to the philosophy of science. And it was a disappointment in one sense that I wanted to study with two people one of whom died, Lakatos, Greek, and a younger fellow, also Greek, which name eludes me at the moment. So, by the time I got there, Lakatos had died, and this young fellow had forsaken the academic world in order to re-join his family enterprise which was Greek shipping, where the money is. Right? I subsequently met him, a very nice and very bright guy. So, it was in that sense a disappointment. But in every other way it was very good. And it was ... I don't know if you know the philosophy of science, but the game as it was played at LSE was that the head of the department who was a devoté of Popper - the department was formed for Popper obviously - and he was defending Popper and everybody else was attacking. And then what you do in philosophy of science is that you take a point, and you take that point in, you prove it or you disprove it. Or you think you did. And you know that was a very useful year, very useful. And in fact that was the year in which I really substantially finished "Theory of International Politics". I did the revisions back here in Maine, but all the basic writing I didn't.

Did you expect the success of the book?
Yeah, I thought the book would be successful. I did not think it would be as successful as it has, but my wife thought it would be a flop, she did not like it.

Did your success effect the people surrounding you?
Well, I suppose it caused the income to go up. So, that was an effect. But my wife is always afraid that I become egoistic or so, she is more inclined to play me down than to play me up, which is a good thing. You could ask her.

Where did the interest in Political Theory come from?
Oh, see ... finally a good sense hit me in the head. I said to myself: What did you really enjoy, when you were in college? And the answer was: literature, and political philosophy. And political philosophy I took was from John Lewis. This is not all, but I mean, John Lewis at Oberlin! And I lived with John and his wife for one semester. And the arrangement was that I did the cleaning once a week and did the dishes and got a free room. And I was able to - see, his wife was then - her book, which you probably don't know, was called "Medieval Thought", published in this country by Knopf and in England in a two-volume edition by Routledge. It's a major work. You know, she knew Medieval Latin just as well as I know English and she had read all this stuff in the original. And sometimes when I was doing the dishes she'd come around, dry the dishes and we could talk about these things.

How did they invite you to their home?
Oh, this is. It was their custom to have a student, usually a senior, living in their house. There's a separate room and a little lavatory and all that. And who would do the cleaning and the dishes, do the cleaning of the house once a week and do the dishes every evening. And because they were both very nice and very, very intelligent, you know, thoughtful, they were real scholars, there were always a few seniors who wanted to do that, I was one of them. Well, it was not a formal competition. But you had to be, you know, they had to accept you.

Did your interest in political thought maybe come from your family?
My family, they had no beans about politics. I mean we'd never talk about politics. And even after I became interested in politics and say: Look it's my field, what do you say? They would not talk about. They would never tell me who they voted for, for example.

Why then International Relations?
Because I got this idea about the three images. Therefore I was typed as being International Relations. And there weren't many jobs. There weren't many jobs period. But there were even less ... to get a job teaching political theory was extremely difficult! To get a job teaching International Relations ... there weren't many of those either, but I was well connected at

Columbia and after spending almost a full academic year, coming back from Korea - I didn't get back until October, which was too late, to start the academic year. So, I had this research job, and then the second year, I still had the research job. But I began to teach one course, a year-long course in International Politics. And then the year after that, I continued to teach the course in International Politics and taught two sections of what is called "Contemporary Civilization" at Columbia, which meant again Plato to the present, but not as political philosophy. I don't know if you ever ... Columbia is famous for this course, it began in World War I as an attempt to get students educated and it was required of all students. It started with the ancient Greeks. But instead of doing a sort of political philosophy what they did was organize the course around whatever movement - intellectual or social political movement - was most important at a given time. So, for example, when we'd get to the era of Newton it was heavily physics. And when we'd get to the era of first development of economics - I don't know if they thought about the physiocrats as they should have, but certainly Adam Smith and John Stewart Mill. It was a wonderful course. I never enjoyed teaching anything more than I enjoyed teaching that one. And it was very demanding. It was a common course, with a common exam. So, you know, somebody you didn't know in economics, you couldn't say: Well, I won't ask any questions about economics but I also won't tell you about economics. Now, it was a common exam, so you had to cover everything. And we had luncheon meetings every week to discuss the readings and make the exams up, it was a nice enterprise. So, I liked that very much. And then of course the kids came along and the public schools were not satisfactory, so we had an opportunity to go to Swarthmore so we took it.

Did this interest in politics and IR relate to some experience?
Yeah, that's right. Because I had this very chequered career, sometimes gone, sometimes ... I had political theory from John Lewis from Plato to Locke, and I thought: Hey, that is fascinating stuff. I did not have Locke to the present because I probably went to Washington that semester. So, in fact, I had almost no spring semesters, I had only the fall semesters, because of the army and various other things. So, I had that from John Lewis and then I went to the University of Texas. I had a course in political theory, Locke to the present, wasn't all that good. But it was interesting. And I took a course in philosophy which was called 19th century thought and I thought, I figured, well that would be Hegel, and Marx and that'd be a great. Well, that was World War II, would be a great background to understand the ideologies. Well, more than half the course was devoted to Kant, probably two thirds, which first I was both dismayed and baffled because I did not understand anything. And this guy who was teaching it was from the University of Chicago and his teaching technique was both posing puzzles and quoting content:

"What do you make of that?". I did not make anything of it at all, until half way through this, and then I became really fascinated. In my view Kant is great. But I would never have found that out if it had not been for this course. So, it's the substance of the intellectual enterprise, which got me involved in these things.

From this your first article developed?
Oh, that little Kant article, yeah. It was 1962 in the Political Science Review. In the PhD dissertation which is called: "Man, the state, the state system and theories of the causes of war", which was not a good title for a book, there was a lot of Kant and a lot of Spinoza. And almost all of the Spinoza disappeared and most of the Kant disappeared when I turned it into a book. And subsequently I thought, well, I write an article about Kant. And my wife and my kids disappeared because my father in law had a heart attack. And they went to North Carolina to be with him for three or four days and I wrote the Kant article. In fact, I started it when they left and finished before they came back and just did nothing but Kant.

So you published this article as a PhD student?
No, no. It was 1962, that was well afterwards.

Would you speak of yourself as a Kantian?
I think of myself as a Kantian, yeah. I went to a Kant Conference at the University of Ottawa, and there were a lot of German scholars, and I gave this talk on Kant. And I said to my wife, Huddie, before I left: This is going to be tough, because there are all these German professors, and I am talking about Kant, they probably cut me to pieces! Did not happen. Did not happen. In fact, I said this to somebody and he said: Ah, German professors, they don't know anything about Kant!

But how does it go together with being a Realist?
Well, Neorealism, or structural Realism. Well, the under-girding is Realism. I consider Kant to be one of the great Realists. He is liberal, but realist. Not contradictory. Have you read Kant? Have you read his political writings? For example, "the mere coexistence of a stronger and a weaker power creates a lesion and under such circumstances preventory war is permissible", that is Realism! It's the mere balance of power. I mean, he is one of the most rigorous Realists. Which is not a contradiction to, I think, his being a political father, the economic father of liberalism Adam Smith, of liberalism. Rechtsstaat, ok. But a Realist, yes, certainly.

22

Kant bridges the gaps between liberal and realist thinking?
Yes.

How did your career develop from then onwards?
See, in Swarthmore. When I was at Swarthmore I had a phone call from Bill Fox saying: The Rockefeller Foundation and Columbia had a programme to finance somebody for a year. And I came up with a proposal, which was in fact the proposal for what turned out to be the second book. And we took the three kids to London and spent fifteen months - an academic year plus two summers - in London, which was a wonderful year for me and the family. We flew over and stayed in a B&B. Well, I went out and looked for a flat, and I found one, on the Abbey road, just a block above the recording studio where the Beatles recorded. There is this song of the Beatles, which they recorded almost exactly where we lived, and it's a very nice part of London. And we had the three kids and the school was founded by Anna Freud, called the 'house on the hill'. It is located after Fencely Road, if you know London. With the youngest and the oldest kid - that was during the summer - in that school and of course when the academic year began. The fall, the oldest kid went to County Council school, which was said to be one of the two or three best in London and I believed that it was a very good school. And the two younger ones were not old enough. So, they stayed in the House on the Hill, which was again wonderful because we could - the school ran from early morning, I forgot what time, until late afternoon - and you could leave them there until noon, you could leave them there until two, you could leave them there until five, you call and say: Well I'm not going to be able to pick the kids up today, keep them. So, we had freedom, my wife and I. We went to Paris and bought a car. We had babysitters, one of whom we are still in touch with. The mother and daughter too lived nearby. We could leave the kids and go to Europe. The daughter was an actress who occasionally actually had a part in a play. You know, actors and actresses are not always regularly employed. We went to see her in one of the plays. For a while she was very well known. And we are still in touch with her. And we knew an awful lot of people, academic and political, because I was working on the second book, Foreign Policy and Democratic Politics. In fact we had a party once, in the late summer of 1960, before our departure, and several MP's showed up, two of them had not even been invited. It was a tremendous party. And as a result we ended up and spent a week in Randall Churchill's house. That's when we were in London for fifteen months.

After you left London, what did you do?
We went back to Swarthmore. Well, overall we were there 9 years, from 1957 to 1966. And two of those years, we spent one in London and another one in Cambridge, Massachusetts in

Harvard. Tom Schelling invited me to come to the Centre for International Affairs and we gladly went, took the three kids again, put them in schools in Cambridge and found a house to rent within a mile of the Centre of International Affairs, so you could walk to the office. See, that's where I finished the Foreign Policy and Democratic Politics book. And we became pretty much full participants because the Department at Harvard was very hospitable. I think, they had monthly meetings, before the meetings they would have cocktails and supper. And they invited me. And after supper when the meeting started of course I left because I was not a member of the department, but I got to know the people at the department very well. I taught a course in American Foreign Policy jointly with Bob Bewey who I've been with at the Law School but who went into Foreign Policy. That was a good experience. The Harvard MIT Arms Control seminar was a flourishing enterprise. And there was this rather large body of people from these two institutions who would meet one time at Harvard and the next time at MIT and it attracted people from both universities plus people from Washington. Military people, intelligence people, foreign service officers, and what not. I gave a talk one evening which became the "Stability in a Bipolar World", published in Daedalus. It was a great group of people, partly because it was both academic and practitioners and because partly it was political scientists and economics people and natural scientists. Steven Weinberg for example, one of the physicists I very much admire, was a regular attender. Obviously very bright, there is no question about that, but also very broad in his interests. And there was Bernhard Brodie who would come occasionally. It was just a very lively bunch. Intellectually exciting, and a lot of controversies. 1963/64 wasn't really the Vietnam war years, but it was the beginning of the Vietnam war years, very controversial, and therefore very exciting. Most people around there were in favour of fighting in Vietnam. That was exciting for me because I was very much against it.

Can you say more about this, why and how you were against it?
I think that is fairly interesting. One is that I had become very ... I had a longstanding interest in China. When I was teaching in my last year in Columbia before going to Swarthmore I taught a year-long seminar for seniors, eleven or twelve students, and I asked myself - I could do the seminar on anything I wanted to do - and I asked myself: What is the most important thing in the world that I don't know much about? And my answer was: China. So, I gave a year-long seminar on China. And among other things we spent a fair amount of time on Mao Zedong and guerrilla war. And this is partly thanks to Ed Katzenbach. When I was in Korea my wife would forward to me issues of World Politics and in one of those issues the lead article was written by Ed Katzenbach. And she would read the things before she sent them and she said: Read this piece by somebody named Katzenbach, it is really good. So, of course, I read it and it was really good and

it was about guerrilla war. When I got back and joined the institute the other principal person at the institute was Ed Katzenbach. He and a co-author, who did not really write it, and I began to read Mao Zedong and to read other things about guerrilla wars as well. And if you do that you learn that guerrilla wars are extremely difficult for outside military forces to win. It is just extremely … It is not impossible, but it gets close. I mean, I know about Malaysia as it was then, but that is an example of how difficult it is, what you have to do. So, that's the one thing. One the one hand you almost certainly can't win this thing. There is a cliché about this: For the guerrillas, if they don't lose they win. For those who oppose them, if you don't win you lose. That really sums it up very, very well. And then the other reason is the international political reason. It did not matter who won or who lost. In other words: the so-called domino theory is nonsense. And if you understand international politics, as for example Henry Kissinger does not, if you understand international politics, you know that the dominoes don't fall. If they begin to fall people get nervous and oppose. I mean, Seoul was a response to the prospect of the dominoes falling. I mean, at international political grounds … Just incidentally Henry Kissinger and Brezhnev both said that the world balance of power is not at stake, in Vietnam, for god's sake! But many, many people in the United States convinced themselves that, you know, the dominoes would fall, and Communism would sweep the world. I mean, that was nonsense. I understand international politics more than enough to know that that was just what it was: nonsense. So, two grounds for opposing it: One is that it does not matter who wins or who loses in Vietnam, for god's sake. And the other is, you probably can't win anyway. So, I began to oppose it in 1963, because you could see it coming. And I can remember one … in 1963/64 when I was at the Centre of International Affairs, there was a good group of military people at the various universities, at Fletcher, at MIT, at Harvard, some at Tufts and Boston University. And they had regular, they had periodic lunches. And they invited me to come and talk. And I talked about the coming war in Vietnam. And I remember the colonel who was sitting next to me and his comment was: Not you too, Ken! Another one is against it. He was a very intelligent fellow. He went on to become chancellor at the University of Pittsburgh, and all that. But the sentiment! Cambridge is Washington and Washington is Cambridge. And when I was teaching at Swarthmore and the Kennedy administration came into office, then they began to import all those guys from Harvard, like George Bundy, and the Swarthmore students were thrilled. You know: Boy, academic university people really being recognized! Becoming highly placed in Washington and have some real influence! I said: Watch out! These guys are academics, they don't know. I mean, they got strong ideas, but no experience. And this is a dangerous combination. Really, really bright people. George Bundy is a very bright person.

What did happen to them?
Oh what happens to them of course is as soon as they get out of public office they become very ... a big wave of common sense washes over them and they disavour everything they stood for when they were in the government. Because finally they had the experience that George Bundy made great sense once he got out of office, but he was a disaster. McNamara, last time I talked to McNamara he was still saying: Mac George Bundy, oh, he was really good, what a mind, a mind like a steal trap! He was wrong! He was wrong about Vietnam he was wrong about the turn. There was a debate: Mac George Bundy versus Hans Morgenthau. And on points I would have to admit that Mac George Bundy won the debate. The trouble is he was completely wrong about the policies that he was advocating. And in fact it was said that his wife was ashamed of it. Because he won the debate as a debater, not as somebody who would talk about what should the country do, what is wise and what is foolish.

Did you get active against Vietnam?
I wrote a piece published 1967 called "The Politics of Peace" which was anti, against the war in Vietnam. And of course I gave a lot of talks about the war in Vietnam, opposing it. I gave a talk at the National Defence College, which is now called the National Defence University, in which I gave a strong talk against the war in Vietnam. I think this is very significant, because obviously the talk was very badly received. And then we had the question period. And the question period I really enjoyed because usually they made their points and I could react to their points. And you know - having been badly received- it tells you a lot about the military at that time: I was subsequently asked if they could reprint a transcript of the speech in their journal. And of course I said yes. And not only did they reprint it, but it was the lead article. Now, I don't think you'd find that situation in the military today. I mean, the military then, much more than the State Department, they … I won't say they embraced their critics but they wanted to hear their critics and were willing to give publicity to their critics. In 1980, I was in Washington with the Wilson Centre, and I was trying to wrap up everything, I did not really want to spend time talking to people in the Pentagon. And I spent one day on the telephone. And I lined up people in the Pentagon to talk to, beginning at 8 in the morning until 6 in the afternoon, including lunch, not a gap. To do that in the State Department is impossible. The military wanted to hear.

But you did not have other opposition?
Oh, I had a lot of opposition, for example from the students. As you know probably from your reading, the people who supported the war in Vietnam early on were better educated, younger, students who were 'gung ho' for the war in Vietnam, college students, until it looked that they

might be drafted. And then they discovered righteousness. This was an unjust war, but they did not know that. Until it looked as though they might be drafted. I did not know about this, but in the Jewish temples they have something called Sunday school. And a major temple, a rich temple, in Brooklyn, MA, asked me to come and the kids discussed contemporary events, cultural, political, social, and the adults had coffee and smoked salmon and cream cheese, it was very good. And then the kids would come in and the invited speaker - in this case me - gives a talk. And I talked about Vietnam. And after I finished the Rabbi who obviously knew his kids stood up and said: Now, I know that Professor Waltz has given you a talk that is very unpopular with you. And he defended my rights to free speech. You know, I did not realize that these kids would go to be so 'gung ho' for the war in Vietnam. But this was very early. And the same thing was true of college students. I remember one time giving a lecture on the war on Vietnam at Berkeley, and the students were so negative. I just made the point that students were gung ho for it until a certain point they might be drafted. And they were saying: That's not true, that's not true! We led the way, we students at Berkeley, we opposed the war. And this TA of mine said: Sure you did! Just as soon as it looked as though you are going to be drafted. Right? Before that: No! And he said he had the same experience. He went to Georgetown, and as a student he was against the war early on. I mean it is a very unpopular position for a student to take to be against the war in Vietnam. It was a worldwide experience. This is one of the things you want to do, you want to teach people to think about their positions.

Did you have a mentor in your life?
I'd said it might be Bill Fox and Bernhard Lewis, but I never took a course from Bill Fox. He came from Yale to Columbia at the beginning of the year and at the end of the year I took the PhD exam. And since I was a minor in International Relations since I thought that not Professor Fox but Prof. Peffer would be the examiner in the minor field and since I was mainly concerned with political philosophy I did not take professor Foxe's course. So, he was not a mentor in the sense of a major intellectual influence on me but he certainly was a sponsor or facilitator, I mean, I do not know what would have happened if he would not have come to rescue me. I mean, I needed a job! And he made it possible for me to spend time doing research and writing. So, I owe him. His wife sometimes uses my office at Columbia. She's about 95. I did not see her last year. Until last year she was coming to faculty colloquia. And she always did the readings, beforehand, asked questions and made comments. But last year she did not make it, so I am wondering. Maybe she is not up to it anymore, which would not be surprising.

Would you have not started an academic career without Professor Fox?
Oh no. My wife and I had decided that when I shifted out of economics into political philosophy, that was the decision.

What came after Swarthmore?
I was invited to join the faculty of Brandeis. And we decided to take the offer. As I said, Swarthmore is a great college, there is no question about that. But we'd been there for nine years and it is small, the student body was then nine hundred, and the system was: everybody in the department, except maybe the chairman, taught a section to the introductory course, which was a terrible course, and then the rest was other seminars. And the other seminars were limited to be seven people, seven students, which could mean eight. But it did not mean more than eight. And I was in the position of having to give two honours graduate seminars each semester on one subject. One semester would be international politics and the next it would be American foreign policy. Well you had two honours seminars, the idea of a honours seminar is that, you know, people contribute papers on a regular basis and you discuss the papers and all that. Well, if you got to give two seminars in the same semester on the same subject it becomes a drain, since you can't remember what you said in which seminar and I got tired of it. So when the offer came from Brandeis I went to visit Brandeis thinking I was not going to go to Brandeis. But after spending a day there I thought, Jesus, it's a pretty exciting place. And we decided to go and we loved it. I mean, my wife loved it, I loved it. We just had a wonderful time. Very interesting faculty and student body, administration, very open place, a lot of arguing. Well, I liked this. But the offer came from Berkeley and, god, it took us a long time to decide. People could not understand, I mean, Brandeis versus Berkeley, obviously you go to Berkeley. We were so fond of Brandeis that is was kind of tough to leave, but we did leave. And, see, despite the many virtues at Brandeis there is one big, big problem, and that is money. The university is underfinanced. This is still the case. The president was great. Although not everybody would agree with that, by any means. But Zacker founded that university and raised the money for that university and then he did a tremendous job in creating the university. I was a great admirer of Zacker's. But anyway, wisely we left because of the money problem. Every time there was a slow up in the Middle East, and you know how frequently that happens, then the money would flow to the Middle East instead of the university. And Zacker couldn't say: Give the money to Brandeis first. He had to say: Give the money to Israel first. And when then there were some left overs: give it to Brandeis. Tough. So, we went to Berkeley. And we were there 27 years.

Did you publish Theory of International Politics in Berkeley?
Yes.

Was it the success from the start?
Well, it got very good and respectful reviews. There is an award given by the American Political Science Association called the Woodrow Wilson prize, and this is what is called the best book in the field, and Theory of International Political came in second. The book that won has disappeared from view. "The System Worked". Well it was about that war in Vietnam and the claim was that the American political system did work. It is an un-claim because somehow the system worked and got us into the war in Vietnam which was certainly ... I mean, I think everybody would say, not everybody, almost everybody would say, it's a tremendous blunder. So, anyway, that book disappeared rather quickly. But it won the prize. Not "Theory of International Politics", but it came in second. And I got good reviews. And, of course, with books in our field, if they don't catch on and become signed in major courses than they have maybe sales of 5.000. 5.000 is considered to be a good sale. So, success depends upon the book being accepted as something that serious students of international politics have to read. And obviously "Theory of International Politics" is one of these books. You have to read it, whether you like it or not!

What was your goal with the book?
The goal was to say some fundamentally important things about theory. I mean, there is theory as theory and then theory applied to international politics. That is why I did all this philosophy of science stuff. Because the word theory is meaningless the way most people use it. So, as I say to my students, if you are going to write - most people do quite a bit of writing - the first thing to do is to learn how. An awful lot of people think that you can't learn how to write. But of course you can. I can teach anybody how to write decent prose, if that person is able to think clearly. But you have to be able to think clearly and you have to care, and you'll learn how to write. If you are going to do theory, the first thing you have to do is to say is: What does the word mean? What's a concept? Which almost nobody got. So, I spent a lot of time. And in fact it does take a lot of time to figure out what the hell a very slippery word like theory means. And I am told now by some philosophy of science people, since almost none of them worry about what the word means, that, yeah, they are coming around a view of theory that's somewhat like mine. To me that is, I am very pleased with that accomplishment. And I think of course I also think I said some important things about international politics.

So is it more about theory?
No, it is "Theory of International Politics". That's what it is. It is theory applied to international politics. It does not take many pages to say what I mean by theory. Doesn't take many pages, because, once you figured it out, you can say it really succinctly. And then of course, is it possible to have a theory of International Politics? We know that Hans Morgenthau said: No, it's not. And Raymond Aron said: No, it's not. He gave us well-known six reasons why you can't have a theory of international politics. And of course, he did not understand what the concept of theory means, nor did Hans Morgenthau. If Cleopatra's nose had been a quarter of an inch shorter, the whole world would have been different. How do you put that into you theory? I've heard him say it. And he thought it was really an important statement. And of course the answer is obvious: you don't. A theory is not about accidentals and peculiarities. You don't put that into your theory. I mean, how do you put the path of a falling leave into your theory? You don't put that into your theory.

Was that the climax of your career?
I would say, yes.

Did it come as a surprise?
The surprise was that it caused most people in the field to say: This you have to take seriously. You better read it. You like it or you don't like, that is a different question. But you have to read it, you have to think about it.

And did this success change your life?
Well, I mean there was that one-year in which I had serious job offers from Michigan, John Hopkins, Princeton, Columbia. All in one year. That was obviously a direct result of "Theory of International Politics". Without that book, I would not have gotten all these offers. I might have gotten offers, but I would not have gotten that many offers from so many first rate places. In fact my wife was so sure that we are going to Columbia that she began to give stuff away to the kids. She said: Well we are not going to take this to the East Coast. When I was offered the fourth professorship - you can´t tell, everybody now has a named professorship in the United States. I mean it´s very hard to find anybody who does not have a named professorship. In those days it was pretty rare. I was the first one to have a named professorship at the political science department at Berkeley. And it meant specifically that I had time for teaching and reading. Full time teaching is two courses per semester and part time teaching is one course per semester. Well, we haven't missed the summer in Maine since 1965. And we like to stay in the fall, because

generally October is the most beautiful month. And people in Berkeley knew that we liked to do that. And they said: Look, if you stay in Berkeley you can teach both of your courses in one semester and you don't have to be here the other semester. That was an informal arrangement; you can't put that in writing. But for all years we were there until the last couple of days or weeks, and the chairman got uneasy about it, because I was supposed to be in, the administration understood it that I would be in residence. But if I chose to, I could teach nothing in one semester, two courses in the other semester. And the department informally understood that it is: I don't have to be there at all. So, that was so attractive to me and my wife that we decided to stay in Berkeley. I took the job in 1971, we did not move there until 1972, that's because we had a kid who was a senior in high school. So, I went by myself and taught. It was a quarter system then and the quarter is ten weeks long. I put all my courses in one quarter and came back to Massachusetts the rest of the year. And then the following year we all moved to Berkeley. And we stayed there until I retired in 1994 at the age of 70. There is no retirement age. You know, we have this crazy system in the United States that there is no mandatory retirement age. I am in favour of that. Except that if you combine it with the tenure system, it is terrible. Because you can have these guys who are well under their seventies who maybe become a bit senile and you can't fire them!

Your 1962 article: Kant, Liberalism and War. Would you consider yourself as a Kantian and as having a connection to Liberalism?
Yeah, I consider myself as a Kantian and I do think I have a connection to Liberalism both through political Liberalism and through economic Liberalism. But, of course, the European terms are appropriate. That means that one is quite conservative. I believe in the largely free enterprise economy, I mean in the Adam Smith way. Adam Smith has a lot of political requirements for the functioning of the competitive economy. And in fact in my edition of the Wealth of Nations I indexed the pages on which he elaborates on the need for political restraints for the competitive economy as going to work properly. So, in that necessarily qualified sense I am a believer in free enterprise hedged about with the necessary requirements and, of course, I believe in a high measure of political freedom. And that makes me an old fashioned liberal.

What is the importance of "Man, the State and War"?
As I mentioned yesterday, when I was doing the heroic reading in the international field to broaden my coverage of it for the examination I found it useful to figure out why so many people then writing about international relations were talking past one another. That is they had significantly different ways of looking at what was going on in international relations. And that

was when I came up with the three images. I think I still have the yellow - and now yellowed - piece of paper on which I wrote the three images down which later became my dissertation. I thought it was a way of making sense of the field of international relations and the different kinds of thinking that going to the interpretation of international relations. That is what I seized upon for a dissertation and after that two-hour exam was over my wife and I did just a few days of a driving tour into New England borrowing her family's car and we talked about this. And that both clarified it and solidified it in my mind. And then I was shipped off to Fort Lee in Petersburg, Virginia, I worked on a prospectus. You have to hand in a prospectus, you probably do this in Germany, you have to hand in a prospectus for the dissertation, and it has to be approved and you go ahead and do the research and writing. So, I did that before I left for Korea. It became my dissertation and subsequently a book.

Has this book shaped the thinking in IR?
Well, it's very widely used. So it must have something to do with what people think about International Relations. I mean, it is hard to find somebody now in International Relations who did not read "Man, the State and War" when he was an undergraduate. So you make the presumption that is has some influence.

Did it lead to research?
I don't know if it leads directly to research. It leads to a way of understanding the field of International Relations, which I think is - in the most general sense - basic to anybody's research. But, I don't think it is a direct influence. "I'm going to do this research project because it follows directly from "Man, the State and War"". Not in that sense, in a much more general sense. All of a sudden, with only a few weeks before the exams - which I could not postpone, because I would go back into the army and it would be a long time, a couple of years, before I could get back to it, and you lose a lot, and I'd sort of would have to start over again studying for the exam. So, I did nothing but read in the field of International Relations, and this in a more general way than I had done previously, and I found all these people saying contradictory things and sometimes very peculiar things, I thought. As reflected in the behavioural science chapter of that book. And my wife did every bit of the research for that. Well, it was not really research, it was reading. And - poor Huddie - she was in Morrisstown, New Jersey, reading this stuff, which is pretty grim reading. And she'd send typed notes to me in Korea and then every once in a while a plaintive letter was saying: Haven't I read enough? Can I stop reading this stuff? It is awful. And, of course, I would say: No, this is fine. This is just what I need. Keep going!

So you developed the idea in cooperation with your wife?
Well, I got the idea. And then we spent quite a bit of time discussing it. Sure.

What else puzzled you about IR at the time?
See, I did not consider myself to be an IR scholar. I was not primarily interested in International Relations. I was interested in Political Theory and I wanted to be a political theorist. But, you had to have two fields, a major and a minor. And, I thought, International Relations would be, perhaps, the easiest minor I could find because I had done work in international economics and it just seemed like a natural transition from economics to politics. You could do it quite easily. But it was a minor interest. So, once I got the idea about the three images it was a nice way of combining some traditional political theory with ideas about International Relations.

In the book you write about the good-evil dichotomy?
You talk about the first image? Those are reflections of course about other people's ideas. But, yeah, it makes a certain - I don't believe in any - in other words, we have become atheists. But by then at graduate school I was an atheist. I was certainly influenced by a really rigorous Lutheran upbringing. Well, you want to know the regimen? It was pretty strict by comparison to other American protestant practices. Of course, as little kid you went to Sunday school and then you went to Sunday school and church. And then in preparation for confirmation we went to Sunday school, church, and Saturday school from 9 to 12 for a year. In which among other things you reported on the previous Sunday's sermon and you had to take notes. And then after a year of that it was Monday, Wednesday and Friday 4 to 6, in addition of course to going to church every Sunday. And you know, we read the bible twice and discussed the memorized verses and all that. It was a discipline, and looking back on it, it was a useful discipline. Even though the religious content in the long run did not take on. It was still a useful regimen to go through. So, and then when it was all over in June, approximately my 14th birthday, we sat in front of the church and the minister asked questions. And each one of the people in turn - we did not speak before the whole congregation - answered these questions that he choose to put to you. And, of course, as a reasonably intelligent person he asked easy question of dumb students and harder questions to smarter ones. But again, it was a useful experience.

Do you believe in the Democratic Peace?
No. There is not any kind of goodness that is going to lead to that result. There is not any kind of governmental form that if you universalize it is going to lead to a uniform result namely peace. Well, I think of the democratic peace as having been a fad. And it was a very big fad, for quite

some time. And there were people who believed so deeply in the democratic peace and believed that it was proved to be true, simply proved! I mean, you could not argue about it. And I think of one person in particular who would get mad at anybody who did not accept democratic peace as a law of politics. I never believed it. I wrote a bit about it in one of the International Security articles saying why I didn't.

Why don't you believe it?
Well, I don't believe that - as Bruce Russett puts it - that democratic peace may transcend Realism. That is that states need not distrust one another. Or Francis Fukuyama: states can live in anarchy and perfect peace! Francis Fukuyama says the same thing: That there is nothing contradictory about anarchy and peace. Well, I think there is. In other words: if the democratic peace theory is right, then "Theory of International Politics" is wrong. I don't think it is wrong. I know a lot of IR people don't think politically, which is a rather saddening thought, but which is true. For example, I think of World War I as being a flat contradiction to the democratic peace. Because I think that Germany prior to World War I was as democratic a state as any major state in the world, including Britain and France and the United States. You know, it had all of the characteristics: The Reichstag had the power of the purse, which is one of the key requirements. If the legislature does not control the budget, then a state is not a democratic state. It had probably the widest suffrage in the world. It had probably the most honest elections in the world, much more so than the United States at that time and maybe since. It had a free and very obstreperous press, which used to drive Bismarck nuts. The largest single party in the state was the Social Democrats party. The Reichstag had to vote the war credits. You know, there were quite a few people who believed the Social Democrats would not - after all those things they have been saying - they would not vote the war credits. But, of course, they did. This was again in retrospect not surprising. I've written about that. There is no such thing as a perfect democracy. I mean, one of the points often made is that in matters of foreign policy the democratic restraints did not work very well. But that was certainly true in England. That was certainly true in France. That just the people chose to blame Germany, the British people, the French people, and Americans, to a great extent. But, I think, not as great an extent than the British and the French. There was the general cross-party consensus in England that you have to keep foreign policy out of the electoral politics, it's an executive function. So, there is not the neat, clear-cut difference on matters of foreign policy between Germany on the one hand and other Western democracies on the other hand. I think, World War I is the classical exception. But you don't win arguments on that ground. I mean, most people have just this fixed view that Germany was not a democracy, Germany being a democracy there wouldn't have been World War I. I mean, that is nonsense.

You know, for example, one of the biggest problems with the democratic peace thesis is that a democracy like the United States if it sees another country that is democratic or more or less democratic and it begins to seem to be going off of track, there is a tremendous temptation to intervene. In the case of the Dominican Republic for example we believe that Juan Bosch - and we accepted that it was as honest and noble an election as you can find in Latin America and probably in the United States itself, we accepted that he was liberal democrat, not a socialist, let alone a communist, a good liberal democrat. We just thought he was too weak to rule. And the CIA identified 17 possible communists in the Dominican Republic. And what did we do? We sent 23.000 troops. I mean, in other words, a military force larger than the entire army of the Dominican Republic. And we did that within one week. It was quite impressive logistically. But isn't that a flat contradiction to the democratic peace? I mean, we liked democratic Latin American countries as long as they are the right kind of democratic American republic and the same thing, even more dramatically, perhaps, is true of Chile. We did not think Allende is being a communist. Never claimed that. He was a social democrat. We agreed. And he was, again, duely elected in a reasonably honest election. We accepted that. We just thought he would take Chile in the wrong direction. That's a big problem. You got a democracy that is not the right kind of democracy going in the right direction. Well, shouldn't we intervene? That was our attitude. They elected the wrong person. In our view. We can't have that. So, you know, where's the democratic peace? Because the United States is so powerful, especially in relation to those Latin American countries, we've got to fight wars.

Did you ever pursue the thought about hegemony further?
Oh yeah, sure. Yeah. I think, first time I did it was 1991 in an article, it was part of what is called the plenary session where the director of that programme for that year asked certain people to give major talks. And there were, I think, three of us, maybe four. Fukuyama was one of them. I mean, the talks were good enough, so that we all ended up being asked to turn the talk into a article. And I was the only one who did not have a transcript and the other guys all were sitting there with typescripts and reading their speeches and I had a few ideas, I gave a talk and it seemed to be pretty good. I reconstructed it and it was called: "America, a model for the world?". And my answer was: No. That the United States was not immune to what had happened to all of the countries who found themselves in a dominant position either in the world or earlier on regionally. And that is if you have a surplus of power what a country does is to abuse it. And this is, as far I can see, true throughout history. And I didn't see any reason to believe that the United States - because it is a liberal democracy - was going to behave differently. And of course it has not behaved differently. It behaved like dominant power always behaved.

What is the implication of dominant power?
It is bad! It is bad for the world. I took NATO as an extended example, the expansion of NATO, and the reason, several reasons, that I chose that was that liberal institutionalists ... see, people like me and like John Mearsheimer said: Ok, the Cold War is over and the United States won. That means the end of NATO. And we both said it, we both said it in print. And, of course, the liberal institutionalists pounced because obviously NATO did not fade away, it expanded. So, I took that as a case to argue that it confirmed rather than refuting what I believed about dominant power. I mean, the Assistant Secretary of State for European Affairs said the expansion of NATO was a way of extending Americas influence and control over European foreign policies. That's the way we looked at it. And I am not aware of any country in Western Europe that was enthused about extending NATO. Helmut Kohl said: Well, it doesn't really matter, does it? It's only symbolic. He said that. He did not say that in public. He said that to a friend of mine privately. When the question was raised about costs - you know what Madam Albright said - it won't cost the United States anything, the Europeans will pay for it, the costs of expansion. Whereupon our wonderful friend Tony Blair said: No, from England not a penny. And was it Chirac? I think it was Chirac, who said: not a centime! I know that there were some Germans who were in favour of the expansion of NATO. But, you know, a rather insignificant minority of Germans. And then we claimed that the East Europeans wanted it. You may recall, we and the Hungarian government worked very hard to get a majority vote in Hungary. The Poles were all for it. I mean, there is no doubt about that. But you can't say - and we do make the blankest statements false - that the East Europeans wanted it. Some did, some didn't. So, why did NATO survive and expand? Because we wanted it to survive and expand. And it illustrates the point: that the dominant powers get their way much more often than other powers do. They don't always get their way. But they certainly have a bit bigger push and a better chance of getting what they want and doing what they want and a greater ability to act unilaterally. Unilaterally and stupidly. Power is not a guarantee of success. We all know that, or should know. But it means you can do things that other states can't do. Maybe they are too smart to try to do them. But you can do those things. I mean, if you want to invade Iraq, you can invade Iraq. A good result is obviously not guaranteed. You know, the neoconservatives now in power hate Realism, because Realists believe over time a balance of power will develop. And they don't believe that. They believe that the United States can be a dominant power and a unique one. Because it can perpetuate its dominance indefinitely. Which is historically and theoretically a very peculiar belief. Historically unprecedented in modern history. I mean, no state has dominated for a very long periods of time. Now, the United States will dominate for a longer period of time than in the past. And some

people take this as an indication that balance of power politics no longer obtains. You know, I think it is very easy to explain why a new balance of power is slow to emerge.

Would you state that balancing is better than hegemony?
Yes. Well, there is no case of the hegemonic powers that has failed to abuse its power. It's an interesting thing in American politics. We believe that profoundly and it applies to domestic politics. The whole message in the constitution and statements in the Federalist papers is to form a system of government with powers checked and limited, and explicitly on the grounds that if power is not checked and limited it will be abused. I mean, it's put very well by Hamilton in a number of Federalist papers and by John Jay in some of the Federalist papers, and of course it is profoundly believed by Madison. He did not write about international politics, but John Jay and Alexander Hamilton applied it to international politics as well as domestic politics. But most Americans don't anymore. Right? It's ok to have dominant power internationally but not domestically. And yet the same considerations apply. That is: the general proposition is that unbalanced power is easily abused.

Which new balance of power will that be?
Well, as of now, it will be the United States, China and possibly India. Not Europe. I mean, Europe has everything it needs to be a great power except for one thing: it doesn't exist. As a political entity it just doesn't exist. It's not capable of ... I mean, European leaders themselves, they can't make foreign policy decisions, you know, if they are important. You can make decisions to give foreign aid to the Middle East or whatever, but if it's a highly political question there is no way of making a decision. It is going to be the lowest common denominator. So, politically and militarily Europe doesn't exist.

Do you think Europe is a 'unit' which could balance the US?
No. It acts on certain questions it can act as a ... but that is not what makes a political unit, right? If you exclude foreign and military policy, you don't obviously have a country. And you are not on the way to have a country. One PhD student at Columbia wrote his dissertation on the question why do some peoples unite and others not. And there is one common characteristic, among those who form a political unity, and that is an external threat. And Europe does not face an external threat. Europe does not face any security worries.

37

Did you already have work on Neorealism in mind when you wrote "Man, the State and War"?
No, as I mentioned, a professor at Oberlin asked me what the sequel was going to be and I said: I don't have any idea. I wouldn't know how to write a sequel. You know, that was 1959, and "Theory of International Politics" was 1979. Twenty years later. Of course, I started working on "Theory of International Politics" well before 1979, it generally takes me a long time to write a book.

Why did the systems perspective in your work become so important?
Almost everybody who writes about international politics thinks of international politics as a system. They just lacked any rigorous way of thinking about it as a system. And the word is really generally very loosely used. So, I set about to answer about the question: what is it that makes international politics a system? How do you conceive of it as a system rather than just a set of interacting units? It did not tell you very much. And in fact most thinking about international politics is at that level of interacting units without any ordered notion of how the system works. What is it in the system that affects the behaviour of the states? It's obvious that the behaviour of the states affects the system, but if you going to have the system, then the system has to affect the states and the states affect the system. And they are part of the system. That's why I developed the notion of structure. Which is the systemic element and it interacts with the behaving units.

Let's talk about theories. Why the interest in theories?
Well, there are different ways of explaining things. Theories are the most general way of explaining things. Some Americans think that theories have to predict. But the key requirement for a theory is that it has to explain. It may also predict. It may or may not. Evolutionary theory doesn't really predict anything. Apart from change, but that does not qualify as a scientific prediction. So, you want to understand and you want to explain and therefore you need theories.

What makes a theory?
Well, it is not a mechanical process. But a theory is a picture of a relevant part of the world, depending on what you are interested in. In other words: a theory has to be about something. It can't be about everything. Even those people, who believe that we will arrive at the final theory, like Steve Weinberger and Steven Hawking. As Steve Weinberger said: When we achieve - and he believes we will - when we achieve the final theory, it won't explain everything. And it may not explain much of anything at all. But it will enable us to understand why things work the way they do. It won't predict - did I say explain? – it won't predict everything, it won't predict much of

anything at all. But it will enable us to understand why things work the way they do. Steven Hawking said: When scientists say "predict" they do not mean "tell the future". That's a quotation. "Tell the future" is not quite the way I would say it, but it is a good way of saying it. You don't mean: tell the future. It is the explanation and understanding of why things work the way they do. That's what theories are after. And to do that you have to, as I say, bound the domain, I mean, it has to be, you can't have a theory of an economy, it has to be a theory of a national economy. Or, it can be a theory of an international economy. But it's not a theory of a domestic polity and economy combined. Nobody has ever figured out how to do that. So, you have got to bind the domain: This is what I am going to try to have a theory about. It is not a guarantee that you can develop a theory. But that is where you have to start. And I go back to the physiocrats who were the first ones to do this. And it is very interesting to read economists before - well, it is very dull, as a matter of fact - to read economists before the physiocrats because they don't have any conception of an economy. And therefore all they can do is what political scientists do: talk about discreet elements. And then you get somebody - predecessor of the physiocrats, I refer to him, William Petty - who is beginning to see: Jesus, I mean, we got all these facts, what are we going to do with them? And, you know, we got a lot of discreet information. But what does it mean, what does it all mean? How do you add it up? Well, you can't add it up just in the way you do arithmetic. You have got to have a conception of a domain that you are trying to understand and trying to explain what goes on inside of it. So, that is the first step. Once you've bounded the domain, than you have just to think: what are the major relations of cause and effect? So you draw a mental picture - just the way the physiocrats – it's a mental picture of an economy or of a domestic political system or an international political system. It explains outcomes, what else do you want it to do?

How do you build theories?
How do you build one? Oh, well, you know. I've just been reading some stuff about Einstein. And he like many other scientists say: I've been thinking about this problem for a long time and all of a sudden, you know, I was sitting there, and all of a sudden I understood. I was sitting in a bathtub, or, I have forgotten who this is, but he said: I went to a movie and it was very, pretty dull and my mind began to wander and I then thought of it. Now, it is obvious, the thought of it means that you've been doing a lot of work on something. It is not just free association. But you've been bothered by something and you've been thinking about something and you've been doing some work on something. And then, you see, hey, now I understand how I can explain it. And nobody can say ... you can't say: I am just going to develop a theory. You got to have work,

preparation, thinking. And then it may not happen, you may never come up with a theory. There are things you probably can't have theories about, it is not admittable to theory construction …

So, it is intuition …
Yeah, sure, I mean, you got to have an idea. I mean, if you don't have an idea you don't have a theory. You can call it intuition. It's not a fact, it's an idea. You can't build a theory mechanically, you have to have an idea.

You speak about the inductivist illusion …
Well, again as Einstein said: There is no route from induction to the construction of a theory. I mean, induction means just know more and more. It is not to say that induction is irrelevant in the construction of a theory. But you can't by induction arrive at a theory. I don't know any serious people writing about this stuff who would disagree with that. Even Jay David Singer, for example, said: We decided to go very far down the inductivist road before we tried to establish a theory. They didn't say: We decided to stick with the induction until we finally got a theory. Because you don't get a theory but just knowing more and more, compiling more and more. As Frank Knight said: every fact is already a theory. Do you understand what he meant by that? That you don't know what is to be taken as a fact. I mean, what some scientists once thought to be important facts turned out to be irrelevant. From the perspective of a different theory that is no longer a significant fact.

Do you use a dialectical approach?
It takes both (inductivist and deductivist approach, CB.). I mean, you got to know some things. Somebody who - well, in international politics, this is a very good example, it goes back to the three images - I mean, those guys were compiling more and more facts that they thought were somehow important in explaining why war sometimes occurs and why other times peace prevails. And the behavioural scientists thought they were on to something. I mean, they had very good psychological techniques, or social psychological, or whatever, within their field, and somehow they naturally believed, and this was especially true as a result of major war, in this case World War II, that we, Jesus, must have something to say in the world about war and peace. And, of course, it turns out that almost none of them did. Because they were somehow dealing deductively with discreet facts. They had no way of connecting them to, no way of figuring out what of all the things that were going on in the world constitute an important part in the explanation of war and peace.

Theories cannot predict.
I didn't say that. I said that theories may or may not be able to predict. It is nice if you have a theory that enables you to predict. But it is not likely in the social sciences that you are going to have theories of high predictive capability. But to have a worthy theory it does to have to enable you to explain. And then maybe predict. And when you predict certain general things in rather gross ways ... again, Jay David Singer said their ambition was to be able to make point predictions, which means you have a theory which would say country A and country B will go to war next Tuesday. I don't think any such theories are possible, in the field social sciences and certainly not in international politics. But we can have, at least hope to have, theories that enable us to explain international political outcomes.

Should theories have normative aspects?
No. I mean, if you say it should have normative aspects I'd say that the theory of gravity ought to have a normative aspect. You know, it'd say: Don't fall out of the windows of high buildings. Right? I mean, who would want that? Who would conceive with that? I don't understand what people mean when they say a theory should have normative aspects or whatever. No. That's not theory.

Did you want to establish a theory already with your first book?
I called it rather lamely - and I realize now - "A theoretical analysis", an uneasy combination with the word theoretical and with the word analysis. But I didn't know any better then. But I certainly thought it had theoretical implications, but I never thought it was in any sense a theory. The book did not pretend to be a theory, it is about theories.

What would you tell scholars engaged in theory building?
Well, first they ought to figure out what they mean by the word theory.

Let's turn to your second most important book. Why is structural Realism necessary?
It was necessary if you are going to have a theory. How can you have a theory without a notion of structure? I mean, again, a lot of national scientists have emphasized that. Gunther Stenz, for example, a molecular biologist said: what is the process of making theories? It is the process of developing an idea about structure, about the structure of the system that you are interested in. Gunther Stenz was a very wise man. He once described the process of building theories as the systematic destruction of information. Meaning, there is an infinite amount of possible information or of possible facts. You got to have some way of destroying some of those seeming

facts, otherwise you got to deal with an infinitude. And you can't deal with infinitude intellectually. You can't. And that is another way of saying that induction is not a route that will lead you to theory, right? So you got to have some kind of an idea, what are the relevant facts for me, for explaining this phenomenon? And that means you have got to destroy a lot of information, you got to destroy a lot of seeming facts. And it's what Gerder meant when he said every fact is already a theory. That is you have got to have some sense of the enterprise in order to know what is to be taken as a significant fact, a fact that is going to enable you to understand this business you are dealing with.

You didn't start as a Realist and tried to reform it?
No. I wanted to understand international politics. That is the beginning point.

However, did you deal extensively with Realism at the time?
From Thucydides, in the Western world, onward the notion about the relations of political entities is based on anarchy. Right? If we are talking about city states, whatever the units are. The common quality is that the relations among them be anarchic, that is what constitutes the international element. You know Bob Gilpin's very nice essay called "Nobody loves a Realist"? I like that. And he is right. You know. People generally don't like Realism. People think that Realists like war, and Realists advocate war. That's just not true. Realists are in fact inclined to understand the grimness of war and want to avoid it. I can't remember … I got this from the reading. When Morgenthau came out as one of the strong opponents of the war in Vietnam, people almost made fun of him because their interpretation was that he is a Realist, he has a reputation for favouring war. And he's got, he generally had that reputation, sort of war like mentality. And now he is tired of that and he wants to become popular. So, it's just a pose that he is against the war in Vietnam. We know he is a Realist, and he is probably for it, but he is pretending to be against it. Which is preposterous.

What is the impact of economics for the development of Neorealism?
Oh, as a way of thinking. Yeah, sure. The microeconomic model, sure. It is built on it, anthropology is like that, and economics, microeconomics, not macro. The system is individually based and spontaneously developed, which is a characteristic of international systems and of biological systems, incidentally, and of economic systems, international political systems. It's applicability is wide. So, wherever you have individualist based, spontaneously developed systems … There is a wonderful multivolume work called "Tour the theoretical biology". I don't know if you heard of it or encountered it. It is edited by Waddington and grew out of a conference. You

42

get a picture of all these people, many of whom were biologists and others who were mathematicians and had something to do with biology. And some of the essays are beyond me, you know, verified scientific essays; but some of them were very suggestive and they were very suggestive because like in international politics biological systems are systems that develop spontaneously, you know, nobody plans them. Except according to the creationists.

So, Neorealism is an economic approach to international relations?
Well, it's not. A lot of people who think would say an economic approach would mean that you elevate economics to a primary position in the conduct of the international politics. No, it's not in that sense, no. Only in the sense of drawing on the theoretical conceptions of microeconomics and applying them and using them in constructing international political theory.

How would you describe your intellectual development from the first to the third book?
Well, "Man, the State and War" was about other people's theoretical approaches, usually not theories, and "Theory of International Politics" was my attempt to build a theory of international politics.

And would you say you have achieved that goal?
Well, yeah, I think that it's a theory, sure.

What are the importance and the limitations of Neorealism?
Well, it explains a limited number of highly important things. For example, the best and most general example is balance of power, why balances of power currently form, why is it balance of power and not balance of threat? Steve Walt was a student of mine and one of my best students, and I think his book is extremely good. But it is not clear to a lot of people, and sometimes I think it is not clear to Steve, that what he was writing about was foreign policy and not international politics. And he says that. Threat is something that statesmen consider when they are forming the foreign policies of their states. Absolutely right. But the theory is balance of power theory because whether or not - many people point this out - states fear the growing power of other states whether or not that growing power constitutes an immediate or short run threat. It is really about balance of power, because if a very powerful state, such as the United States is now, pursues a benign foreign policy for a time, because it is in a position of having unbalanced power, you don't know what it is going to do in the future. And this is a reversal of what people like Keohane and Axelrod say, who think of the shadow of the future as being something that promotes peace. If you act under the shadow of the future you know that the

move you make today has implications for tomorrow. The shadow of the future is more generally a cause of war. I would say the shadow of the future was in the most general sense the cause for World War I. For everybody the war was a preventive one. And prevention is a very common response to the uncertainties of international politics. Not pre-emption, but prevention.

How do you think Neorealism was improved in the following?
Oh, oh. Important contributions! I don't want to accuse people of being structural Realists who may not consider themselves to be either structural or Realist. But nevertheless lots of people made contributions. Gilpin is obviously one of them, Bob Jervis is obviously another, Glen Snyder, who is, I think, much underappreciated, is another one, John Mearsheimer, Steven Walt. Sure, there are a lot of people …

Will Neorealism remain the dominant paradigm?
Well, it will remain so until somebody comes along with something that impresses the relevant community of scholars as being the better way of viewing international politics. I can't quite see what that development would be. But, one knows that from contemplating the development in other fields that the dominant way of thinking. You know, Newtonianism gives way to Einstein's conceptions of the world, without becoming irrelevant. You know what physics is used in the space programmes: of course, Newtonians. It's not Einstein's. Einstein is just too complicated. You have got to solve too many almost impossibly difficult equations. As long as you know where the moon is going to be in a given time and you want to put somebody on it you don't need the precision that Einstein would give as compared to Newton, you just shoot at the thing, and there it is.

What was the most important criticism to Neorealism?
Well, it is hard for me to say what the most important criticism is. I think, of course, that most of the criticisms are misplaced. Joe Nye kind of: you've left something out!. Keohane! Keohane and Nye described their enterprise in their book Power and Interdependence as trying to come up with a model that would correspond more closely to reality. Well, that's medieval science! When do I want to go back to King, Keohane and Verba, they are cracked on reality. I mean, how do you test a theory? You put the theory up against hard empirical fact. Well, I think, if we knew what hard empirical fact is, what we need a theory? It would make theory irrelevant! Where are the positivists? Let's just look at the facts for god's sake and see if your theory corresponds with those facts. That is exactly how modern science did not develop! You take very long steps away

from reality in order to develop an instrument called theory that would enable you to explain, sort out the facts, discard some. And every fact is already a theory.

So you don't agree with theory-testing?
Oh, theory testing is very difficult and very problematic. I don't agree with Lakatos about everything and he is certainly very poor on the question of theory. Now, he said: Take a theory, such as: all swans are white. How could anybody think of all swans are white as a theory? It does not qualify as a scientific hypothesis! I mean, it has nothing to do with theory. But Lakatos is very good on testing. As he said: there is no way of proving a theory true, but then there is also no way of disproving a theory. Tests are never conclusive. Because, as another philosopher of science puts it, the background information against which you are testing your theories are themselves very problematic. How do you know it is an empirical fact at all? Let alone a hard one, or whatever that means. Most people think if a theory is not disprovable it is not a theory, or a so-called theory. If it is not disprovable it is not a theory. This is not true. Most natural scientists spent most of their time trying to show that theories are valid. But we spent most of our time showing that they are false. That is one possible way of going at it. But the philosophers of science make the point that by and large you don't try to prove a theory false, you try to verify it. Use it. Right? And we know how problematic this is because there is no possibility of finding a body of theory that was tested and applied in more varied ways than the Newtonian system. And yet, in the end, it turned out it is not a sustainable theory. And there are people, of course, who are saying the same thing about Einstein. You know, the system is not closed, there are problems with it. So that's the story of science. If you had a closer and closer correspondence to reality you would not have theory. I have talked to Keohane - we are friends - about this and he calls my theory parsimonious, and sometimes too parsimonious. And I say: What you are saying about it when you are saying that, as you are saying it, is a theory? There is no such thing as a theory that is not parsimonious. And the theories that impress us are very parsimonious indeed. They leave almost everything out. Then along comes Joseph Nye and says: Oh, you left something out! Information flows, information flows are not in the theory! I don't even know what the hell he means about information flows in that context! Demographics are left out. I mean, of course! Theories are mostly omission. As soon as you read Joseph Nye, you know he does not have a clue about what the word theory means. Therefore he makes this criticisms that makes him sound dumb. But a lot of people, I am sure, are impressed

Would you like to reconcile your theory with others?
Why would I want to do that? I don't see that as even a possibility. I mean, a theory does have to have inner coherence, or it's not a theory, of course. A lot of people do write about theory in that way. You left something out, this is an important variable, and it is not in your theory, better added to your theory. You can't do that! You can't just plug a variable into a theory, there is a completely different notion of what the word theory means. If somebody thinks that, well, he left a variable out lets just put it in and then we would have a better theory. The theory wouldn't explain more. You won't have a theory at all, because, a theory is a very simple. And simple is what people mean when they say a theory is beautiful. As Steven Weinberg said about Einstein's early work, it was paralyzingly beautiful but full of errors. Well, what does beauty have to do with the errors? The beauty is in there like it is the simplicity of the conception, not the complexity of those damned equations you have got to solve, but the conception. And Einstein himself emphasizes that, Weinberg emphasizes that. It is the simplicity of the conception. Which I don't find very simple. But natural scientists do.

Why are your units states?
Well, that's an empirical question. Are states the most important units in international politics or are they not? To say that they are the most important units is a factual statement. So it's disputable. So, if somebody comes along and says: No, no, no, nongovernmental organizations are the fundamental units. That is an empirical contest. Which is more important: non-governmental organizations or states? Informing the international political system? Well, I think it is a non-argument, but that is the level at which the thinking would have to take place. If states are not the most important units in the international political system, what are the most important units? I don't think there is any answer that could stand up against the state. But it is a factual statement, so you can dispute it.

So what about NGOs, for example, are they completely ignored?
Sure. Sure they are. Now, they are completely ignored in the theory. Now, you know, people confuse this sort of thing, there are a number of criticisms saying that: Realists in their accounts leave out the differences across states. Well, in their accounts nobody leaves that out. The theory does, but there is a confusion about Realists who are trying to explain and give an outcome and who use the theory plus facts, plus what they take to be facts, the theory plus information about the situation that obtains. I mean, there is no such thing as a theory that gives you the answer. A theory does not predict, I may predict. But the factual empirical information that you need in

order to explain a given situation that is not in the theory. How could it be? Theories are very sparse, simple, parsimonious.

What would you argue against the withdrawal of the state?
Well, it's just not true. Well, states change. Now, in what direction? In the direction of doing more, intervening more in every aspect of society. We know that, you see that if you simply compare the level of governmental spending. That is how much of the gross national product is the government appropriate, now as compared to earlier times. Well, we know that around 1900 governments did very little. The police functioned, delivering the mail, right, it did not have a big role to play in matters of income distribution, in matters of health, human welfare in general. Governments were more external actors, in foreign policy, military forces, and all that. And they did relatively very little, domestically. Now they take a big chunk of the gross national product. Even a country like the United States, which is a low taxation country, takes a lot more of the gross national product than it did, say, around 1900. I mean, it's just no comparison. So, yes, the states become more and more powerful and more and more important. And then people who must know this - the increased sphere of activity of the states - will say: oh, the states are fading away! Other actors are becoming more important. States are becoming less important. That's bewildering. It's bewildering. How can anybody believe this? It just goes against everything that has happened and is happening. And in fact, people know that. What was the Thatcherite movement: we got too much government, right? The government is not withering away, it has become too much of a factor in one's daily life and in social life generally. So, you have to reduce the government! Soviet Union, yes, Thatcherite England, yes, Reaganesque America, yes. Too much government, get rid of it! And then these people say the governments are withering away! Well one of these things is supposedly terrorism. We had a panel, which was picked up by C-Span, which means that nobody saw it. It had Tom Friedman of the New York Times, Tom Shelling, and I was on it, and I think that was it. And we went on for a couple of hours, had a big audience. And one thing we all agreed, we did not even discuss it, one thing we all agreed incidentally was that terrorism makes the state more important. But a lot of people would say … Joe Nye, for example, you can also rely on Joe for these things, that now terrorists can organize power and dispose of it on a scale that even middle ranking states can't reach. Absolutely false, this is absolutely untrue! They can't. They can't use force in a way that makes it possible for them to sustain the use of force. Isolated blows, yes, very annoying, yes. But they can't sustain the use of force. They can't use force and then occupy a territory and then sustain themselves within it. Isolated blows, that is what they can do. Which can be very serious. But it is not on a level of what states can do. And the more terrorist threats there are the more people look to the state to

protect the people. And the predictable result - and I wrote this immediately after the thing occurred - I said, of course the government will use the threat of terror to increase its own powers. It enabled the Bush administration to do just exactly what it wanted to do. Only now after the Twin Towers and all that, the Bush administration could do it much more easily. For example, withdrawing from the ABM treaty would have been a matter of sustained dispute. We were able to do it just like that.

Why is power so important?
Well, in an anarchic system each unit has to protect itself the best it can. And power simply is a word that stands for the means of enabling states to do that to a greater or lesser extent. So, it is inferred directly from the theory about the conditions of international politics. The power is the basis for states existence. It is a combination of the attributes that states have to have in order to be and remain states. It is not a single factor, the most general factor is political competence. So, it has to have a certain level of political competence. And if it doesn't, for example at the end Tsarist Russia it did not have, then it's going to suffer, as Russia did. It is going to suffer grievously. But political competence, demographic strength, economic strength, technological capability, I mean, all those things are going into what we call the power of the state.

What about soft power?
Ah, well, soft power. Nye does make this point, of course. Soft power follows hard power. If you got hard power you got soft power. Who had soft power in the 1930ies and again in the 1950ies, what country? The Soviet Union! John Kennedy's slogan with which he won the elections in the 1960ies was "get the country moving again, the Russians are coming!". There was a movie which my wife and I enjoyed immensely which was called "The Russians are coming". People believed, and Jack Kennedy believed, that the Soviet Union was catching up with and, it was just a question of time, would surpass the United States in economic and technological capabilities, unless we did something. Let's get the country moving again. Right? And you had countries in Africa saying: Hey, look at us, we are socialist, we are socialist countries, send aid! It's this pitiful pretence that an African country had the ability to being socialist in any sense. But nevertheless the Soviet Union was, it looked as though it was becoming a dominant, maybe the dominant, part of the world. Same thing of the 1930s, the major country with the highest industrial growth rate in the world was the Soviet Union. Or think of E.H. Carr, the first edition. His version of Realism was "Who's rising, who's falling". Well, Italy, Germany, the Soviet Union, right? Directed economies, fascist systems. I mean, they are rising, the democracies are sliding downward. So, what is the realistic response to this? Join the winners! Don't fight them, join

them, right? This all disappears in the second edition. In the preface to the second edition E.H. Carr says: Well, I've made certain changes to clarify my positions and improve the prose. He was not only an appeaser. He wrote the lead editorials for the London Times, advocating appeasement of Germany and Italy.

Why do states in Realism have to defend? Why is there no room for cooperation?
There may be under certain circumstances, sure. And alliances are of course ways of cooperating, but they are militarily based. I mean, that's cooperation: to increase the strength of the cooperating collectivity against possible incursions from abroad. You know, if you are perfectly secure you wouldn't have to worry about security. Doesn't mean you won't. It is hard in modern history to think of a state that faces fewer and less serious threats to its security than the United States does now. But that does not seem to lead us to pacifist policies, which we could very well afford to follow! And we'd be much better off if we did. We'd be obviously better off, we'd spend less on the military, we spend as much or more as the rest of the world combined. Why? We don't face and external threat that is worthy of our efforts. But we continue. I mean, it is pitiful. It's not strange, it's not unexpected.

Regarding a pacifist state, is this possible?
Oh sure. Stefanie Newman, at Columbia, office next to mine, edited a book written by a number of different people who were specialists in what I might call peripheral countries, you know, South East Asian countries. Her message is that not everybody thinks like a Realist. And not all leaders of states or populations of states think in terms of security. They think in terms of other things. So, it is perfectly possible. And historically true in some cases. But what happens to those states? Oh, ordinarily they get overrun, they get conquered. India is a wonderful example. Wave after wave people were coming in to India, taking over. And even Nehru was shocked when the Chinese invaded. It was largely India's fault, in my view, in 1962. When there were prolonged negotiations over the disputed borders and it is fair enough to say that the Indian's really stonewalled, they thought they were in a strong position and they would just hold and the Chinese would have to give up sooner or later. And the Chinese got fed up and invaded. And Nehru said: This is astonishing. This is the last thing we ever expected. Yeah, you can behave like a Nehru. Perfectly possible. It's just that your country is likely to suffer. It is not sure. You might get away with it. But you got to - and at least in retrospectively say - ok, that was our policy and that caused our suffering. And then of course typically Nehru panicked. I mean, remember where this takes place, in one of the most inhospitable parts of the world in October! So, the Chinese have got to go somewhere? No, it was border rectification, it was obvious to anybody looking at

it from the outside that this was not going to be a prolonged major invasion and war, but having neglected the defences that the state relied on. Intelligence and good will and cultural understanding and all that. Having relied on those weak reeds and then one day suddenly the reeds break, crack! Not a good way to run a country.

Can anarchy be overcome?

No. I mean, a world government? How else can you overcome anarchy? Fortunately impossible. Well, the United States are not going to conquer the world. If a country became powerful enough to do that we might have a world government, that is, a government imposed by the dominant power. Not most people outside the dominant power would like that and a lot of people inside the dominant power wouldn't like that. It's not a world government that people have in mind. But how would a world government come? Try to think of a government in form, or a country that would form out of many into one. It is almost impossible. I can't think of any case in which this happened without strong pressing external threats. The United States may be the best example of where the threats had to be greatly exaggerated, in order to get the result. But that in a way makes the result. You got to make enough people - in what is going to become the state - you have got to make enough people believe that their only means of becoming secure is to unite. You can't do that on a worldwide basis. What was the name of this Frenchman who wrote the book translated as "The Next war is the War against the Moon"? The message was: until there is a threat from outer space we are not going to have world government. If there is a big enough threat from outer space, that might do it.

What about the United Nations, Global Governance?

Well, you don't relate things to your theory. You could infer from the theory that the United Nations is going to be as important as the major units within the United Nations want to make it become. And the international institutions are created by the more powerful or the most powerful state for the benefit for the more powerful or the most powerful state. You know, the expansion of NATO is an example of that. It happened because we wanted it. We wanted it because we thought it would serve our purposes. I think we were wrong, but that doesn't qualify the fact that it was done by us to serve our purposes. The United Nations was set up by the more powerful countries, the position of the more powerful countries was protected by the veto, it's run by the more powerful countries. And again in the case of the first war in Iraq we had the imprimatur of the United Nations, so we used that, we build a coalition and all that, that's fine. And then with the second war in Iraq, we did not have the approval of the United Nations, and we said: To hell with it, we are going to invade Iraq because we want to invade Iraq. We don't care what the United Nations say.

So, this kind of cooperation is always formed as a defence against external threat?
NATO does not have an external threat. It was originally. We know Bernhard Brodie in 1973, it was quite a while ago, he said: NATO was important, NATO served an important function. Now, it's obsolete. It's no longer needed. How do we get rid of it? It's one of the institutionalists, they like institutions. They never take up the question: How do you get rid of them. We should have gotten rid of NATO long ago.

How do you explain then that it is still there?
Well, it's pretty easy to explain. You know, organizations perpetuate themselves. They want to perpetuate. It is very hard to kill organizations. One of Keohane's favourite examples is the March of Dimes: One of history's most successful organizations, it set out to extirpate polio and it succeeded, that is a tremendous accomplishment. But did it go out of business? No. You got the organization, right? And the organization wants to perpetuate itself. You got to find something else to do. It was very difficult because all of the best diseases were taken. Cancer? That was gone. That brings a lot of money. Heart? Lungs? All those things were covered. So, it ended up with birth defects. Not nearly as diverse as, say, cancer. But it perpetuated the organization. Now, NATO is different. Because NATO is a treaty among states. So, it isn't that just the organization as an organization perpetuated itself. They required a state - it could have been two or three states, but in fact it was one - that wanted to perpetuate the organization. And that was us. And as I said before, the Assistant Secretary for European Affairs said: We want to retain NATO as a way of extending our influence over European foreign and military policies. That is not an exact quote, but that's the gist of it. Sure. Now, he ought to have been smart enough not to say that out loud. But we would know anyway. You know, it is like Thucydides. He didn't hear all those speeches, but he said: given the circumstances what is it that the leaders in this particular instance would have said? How would they have been thinking? Well, we know, we can figure that out even if the Assistant Secretary had not have pointed that out: That there was one country that wanted to perpetuate and expand NATO and that country was powerful and powerful countries often but not always get their way. Why should Germany or England or France oppose the expansion of NATO? They can only lose. And the United States has more favours to dispense and more penalties to impose on other countries than anybody else does. So, you don't want to oppose the United States unless it is really important to oppose. You know, when we invaded Iraq for the second time, the Germans and the French uttered their disapproval

but they did not sustain it. Because they know they can't win. So, why do it? You are just going to make the United States mad.

Do you think there is a possibility that alliance formation takes place due to internal threat?
Well, it's a possible tactic, yeah. It isn't likely to work. It is hard to think of. You see, Britain and France were always deeply sceptical about each other, they didn't trust each other, the more democratic both countries became during the 19th century the more they distrusted each other. Right? So, ordinarily what brings two countries together - Britain and France, France and Russia are very good examples, countries who distrusted and disliked each other deeply. Think of the French and Russians after the revolutionary Napoleonic wars invasion of Russia by France. I mean, those historical memories run deep. To bring France and Britain together required the perception of a grave external threat. That's ordinarily how alliances are formed. Can you think of an instance were two countries that were adversaries and not great threats to each other made alliances?

France and Germany after World War II ...?
After World War II? Well, that is not a very good example. See, again, we know this historically that when one country ceased to be a major power they behave differently. And Germany and France and England were demoted. It took them a while. It took Britain and France a while to come to terms with the fact that they were no longer great powers, the fact that they weren't. They became, in League of Nations terms, consumers of security rather than providers of their own security. ... (n.u.) puts this very nicely, comparing the Western European situation, comparing the French and German situation with Rome and Athens. He said: To contemplate a war between Germany and France would be as boring as it would have been to contemplate a war between Athens and Sparta in the days of the Roman Empire. They'd become side shows. They might quarrel, they might even fight. But who cares? I mean, in the system this is not really important. And France and Germany and Britain were reduced to the status of major powers, not great powers. Which puts them into an entirely different situation. They can come together, they can cooperate with each other. You see, they don't have to worry about relative gains. Because they are not capable of ensuring their own security by their own efforts. So, they don't have to worry about relative gains. So, they could do things they couldn't do when those countries were great powers. In other words, it is easy to explain when you are a structural Realist. It's easy to explain: The structure changed.

What is the role of unipolarity?
Realist theory in general and structural theory specifically is a theory about how two or more states interact in a condition of anarchy. And you don't have two or more states interacting anymore. So, much of what you infer from structural theory is no longer true. In other words, there is not a countervailing state. There is nobody to moderate the behaviour of the United States. So, what the United States chooses to do, its internal politics, its internally generated and the implications become much more important and the international constraints become much less important. That is what it means to be a dominant power. That is why it is so dangerous. That doesn't mean there are no constraints whatsoever in the international political system. But there is not the direct kind of moderating behaviour that the United States and the Soviet Union did.

We stopped with France and Germany and why they could become friendly and not fear one another. The structure changed and therefore their behaviour changed. Because they are no major powers they don't have to balance?
Right.

How can Neorealism explain the end of the Cold War?
Well, the Cold War was a relation of antagonism between the two principal countries in the world and one of them disappeared. As I wrote in an article, the Cold War is rooted in the structure of international politics and will only end when this structure changes. It's exactly what happened.

Can it explain 9/11?
Why would you expect it to explain 9/11. It can't. I mean, there are some obvious things. It used to be, when there were two great powers, weak people could hope to play one off against the other. They can no longer hope to do that. There is nobody to play off against the United States, which lends to a certain desperation, striking out in the theory. I wouldn't say that is directly inferred from the theory but the theory helps you to understand that. But that's about all one can say.

So the theory doesn't include actions of sub-state actors, but is it only on superpowers?
No. Well. It applies regionally. If you have a certain numbers of regional countries contending within a region it would apply to them and within a region, sure.

What can Neorealism say about globalization?
Well, sure. Globalization is not globalized. Globalization is Americanization. Interdependence is about the dependence of most countries on the United States, which the United States chose to call interdependence for obvious reasons. Interdependence became the American ideology and used to make foreigners mad. As Jeffrey Goodman said, interdependence is an euphemism used by Americans to disguise the dependence of most countries. Right? Most countries depended on the United States, but the United States did not depend on them. And Suez was a wonderful illustration of that, where the United States could turn on its two major allies – Britain and France – and dispute them, as Eisenhower did. We cut Britain off, and Macmillan came to heel, quickly. There was no American money, no possibility of sustaining a war in the Middle East. And the British and the French as well learned that immediately. But you couldn't do that. In a multipolar world it would not have been possible to do something like that. The German-Austro-Hungarian connection is a perfect illustration of that. Germany could not - even when the Kaiser disagreed with the Austro-Hungarian ultimatum to Serbia - he could not forsake Austria-Hungary and therefore he could not discipline Austria-Hungary. But we could discipline our major allies.

And this applies to today's world as well?
Well, it is no longer a bipolar world, now it's a unipolar world. So it does not apply perfectly and literally. You know, we don't have allies. In other words, we don't expect them to come to our aid militarily. They may expect us to come to their aid militarily. Is that an equal relation? The word alliance no longer means what it used to mean in a multipolar or even a bipolar world. Entirely different. Because the structure has changed.

Will there be peace when the system is unipolar, bipolar or abolished?
Well, I don't think there is ever going to be universal and perfect and reliable peace whatever the system, whatever the characteristics of the system.

Not even if there is a world state?
I am a Kantian. You know what Kant says about world government. It would be the greatest tyranny the world has ever seen. In the end it would dissolve and there would be civil war and you'd be right back to where you started. Except you would have gone through a very messy and costly - grossly enlarged - process. I think that is true. I mean, if you are thinking of a world government as the UN with a few sharper teeth, well, that is not world government. We know what is required. It is the same old story. The greater the individuality of the units in the system and the greater the diversity the stronger the central government has to be. This is the age old

pairing of highly individualistic societies and very strong rules. This is a common historical pattern. Well, if you imagine a government over the states, and the states are themselves, some of the states are themselves very powerful and certainly diverse, so we would have a tremendous power at the centre. And if you have a tremendous power at the centre you have something to fight about. Who's going to control the controllers? Well, that is about as far as you need to go. It would, as Kant said, be the world's greatest tyranny. If it would be a functioning government. But most people talk about world government ... Hans Morgenthau talks about world government, Alexander Wendt says world government is inevitable, and it is not a possibility, it is an inevitability. They don't really ask themselves what a world government would have to be, what powers it would have to have.

Let's stay with Alexander Wendt and his different conceptions of anarchy.
Anarchy is what you make of it? Yeah. Peculiar. Because, you know, the 'other regarding'. You can't behave in other regarding fashions, I mean, that's the alternative: the 'self-regarding' is 'other regarding'. So, I don't act for myself, I act for us or the collectivity. Well, it's pretty hard to know what I'm supposed to do if I'm acting for the collectivity and your idea and my idea what is appropriate to do were going to be different. So, you can't get out of this self-regarding, I mean, you can only be other regarding if you have absolute assurance that you are going to be taken care of. Properly, by your standards. And there is not any possibility to achieving that. And Alexander Wendt often makes that clear. I have a rather high regard for Alexander Wendt, that doesn't mean I agree with him. I certainly think he's the best of the people writing in that vein, Constructivism, he is far and the way the best and that is of course why a lot of Constructivists don't like him because he is not Constructivist enough. He sees the difficulties. He sees the problems with it. You see, the term he uses, it is not ideas all the way down, there is a reality. We corresponded briefly way back when we were in London and that probably had been in the early 1990ies and he said - he was teaching in Yale - he said that some of the students in Yale asked him sometimes: Where is it that you and Waltz really disagree? There is quite a bit of agreement between us. That is because he is a very guarded Constructivist. He understands that there is a reality, you have to deal with it. Anarchy is not something what you make of it. He believes that one way and doesn't believe it in many other ways. You are not free to be just other regarding. You are not free because there are a lot of constraints on you that arise from anarchy.

Would there be a Kantian anarchy?
Anarchy is anarchy. Just as Realism is Realism. I don't see why you need to modify Realism with words like defensive realism or offensive realism. I disagree with ... I generally agree with

Mearsheimer, I have a very high regard for him, but I don't really believe that he is an offensive realist. And I don't believe that as he claims that he derives this position without any assumptions about human nature, that it's purely structuralist. Conclusion: he claims. I don't see how. I mean, to put it very simply, offensive realism would mean that the offensive strategy is always the right strategy. I don't believe that. I don't see how anybody can believe that. And I don't think that John believes that. Because, he does put the stopping power of water, which is both suggestive and puzzling. Because, when you think of water you think of transportation. You think of transportation as means of violence, as well as goods and people. And the British Empire is certainly a case of - and so is the American - that is: airpower, sea power, we can act very effectively in long distances. So, the stopping power of water from the Portuguese onwards did not stop very effectively.

You write in one article that the growing inequality will lead to instability.
Well, sure. In order to balance, these people who claim the end of balance of power politics or even a greater extreme: transformation of international politics. Transformation again is a word that is used very loosely. Some people say it has already been transformed. Interdependence, globalization, whatever. If international politics were transformed it would mean that nothing that we have ever heard or believed about international politics any longer remains true. If some of the old ideas do remain true, then international politics have not been transformed. I think, you know, it is obviously wrong to say that it has been transformed. Or will be. Now, that means balance of power politics still works. But balance of power politics never does work, or almost never does work very well. I mean, think of World War II. A balance did not form completely until after the war started. First, the Soviet Union and then the United States remained detached until 1941 and effectively until 1942, obviously, and that is well after the war started. Americans tend to say the war was starting in 1941, December 7. The Europeans don't, right?. So, that's just one of many illustrations of how balancing is expensive and dangerous. Not balancing is dangerous and in the long run often more expensive, but balancing requires positive acts. It is not, well, Britain and France just not getting together, Britain, France and Russia not getting together. It is not negative, it is positive. You got to do something. And that means bearing expenses. And they are not simply economic expenses, they are political expenses and they may be military expenses. When Stanley Bolton was asked why he did not advocate disarmament, his answer was very simple. If I had done that we would have lost the elections of 1936. He's probably right, they would have lost the elections of 1936. And what's more important? Building up your strength in the face of a threat from Hitler or winning the elections? Well, most political leaders are going say: Winning the elections. We have to win the election first. Then we can do

other things. These people who say balance of power politics is obsolete, and point to the fact that ... you see, balances ought to form because of the United States behaving very arbitrary, in a highhanded and dangerous fashion. But always before when great wars ended, the materials for balancing were left in existence. We know after the French revolutionary Napoleonic wars how quickly a balance was reconstituted. How France was taken back into the system for the sake of balance, all that. You had enough great powers standing to form a new balance of power. This was true after World War II, when forming a balance was no problem at all, it was a given. If you only have two countries, the balance is going to be between those two countries. And then some people say: Yeah, but suppose the other country had been Britain, then that would have been different. I don't agree. It would have been different. But still it would have been a balance between the United States and Britain rather than the United States and the Soviet Union. We know that, although a lot of people don't admit it, because of the rift that developed between Britain and the United States throughout the end of the war on the question of imperialism. If Britain had survived World War II as a great power it would have been Britain with its Empire. And it wouldn't have been the same content as between the United States and the Soviet Union, but the major tension would have run between the United States and the British Empire. And then, at the end of the Cold War, there was just one country. So, of course, it is going to take a lot longer. And combining is always inefficient. One plus one does not equal two. One plus one equals one plus, not two minus. Now that is even more true. As De Gaulle always said: Nuclear weapons don't add up. You know, if I have a second strike force and you have a second strike force, and we ally, what do we have? We have a second strike force. We don't gain strategic dominance. And this is obviously true with nuclear weaponry. But it is also true now with increasingly complex systems of surveillance, logistical systems. At one point, when Britain offered more help in Afghanistan - this was before the war in Iraq - we rather rudely rejected it. Rumsfeld's notion being: god, it's hard to combine. Their logistic system with our logistic system, their surveillance system with our surveillance system. It is hard enough among the different services in our country. When you cross countries ...

How is the change from unipolarity going to happen?
How is it going to change? China. The only thing that could stop China would be political conflict within China, and some people have speculated about that. That is the booming coastal areas and the interior of China, which is like way behind. We travelled quite a bit of China and the contrast between the coast and the interior is stark. But I don't think it's going to result in political dissolution. It is a problem, but it is not serious enough. So long as China remains fairly coherent as a country it is on the route to challenge the United States and it has good reason to

challenge the United States. By challenge I mean: put itself in a strong enough military position so that we cannot simply act unilaterally. And, of course, the immediate concern for the Chinese is over Taiwan. It is hard to realize how important it is to the Chinese until you really talk to one of the Chinese. All kinds of all very Western oriented Chinese - we will call them real democratic -, you talk to them about Taiwan, their views are really remarkably uniform. One of these guys said – he's got a PhD from Berkeley and he's well established in China, teaches at Peking University, his wife is a very successful owner, manager of a hotel - and you talk to him about Taiwan, as he put it to me one time: Well, first it is Taiwan, then it is inner Mongolia, then it is Tibet, then it is Saint John, and what is left of China? Dominoes! The first domino is Taiwan. And then: Whoosh.

When multipolarity is going to replace unipolarity, what are the effects?
Oh, we will be right back in the good old international politics. We won't have a dominant power. We will have two or more major powers in the world, and we know about that. I mean, to get from here to multipolarity, one would expect bipolarity to be the first step, and we know how bipolarity moderates each other's behaviour, this was true of the United States and the Soviet Union all during the Cold War. Again, Americans don't think that the behaviour of the Soviets was very moderate during the Cold War, but if you look at it from a larger historical perspective, then, you know, it really was. I wouldn't want to argue this very strenuously with East Europeans. But we had our sphere. The whole world was not occupied or strongly influenced by the Soviet Union. The Soviet Union had its sphere, wherever the influence of the Soviet Union did not extend, we moved right in. And we continued that. Now of course that we are the sole superpower we move in all the more and all the faster. I mean, we've got China surrounded, we've got Russia surrounded, we got so many bases we can't even count the number of bases we have! Certainly over 350. Now, you are getting the problems of counting because there are weather stations, there are radar stations, do you count those as bases or don't you? You know, what makes a base? But we got hundreds and hundreds of bases abroad. And then, one of the worries about Iraq is that we establish ourselves in that whole part of the world with our bases and Uzbekistan and some of the others. It's what dominant powers do.

How do you describe the hegemony of the US? Is it an Empire?
Oh, sure. I mean, it all hinges on how you define empire. But, I mean, certainly, there is probably a better way of conveying what is happening by not using the word empire. But I accept that. I think our behaviour ... I mean, if you do a profile of imperial nations, we fit the profile pretty well. In major and minor ways. I mean, the peace-corps was the secular equivalent of sending

missionaries abroad during the British Empire. And just as the British trained the distant people by training their military officers in England, we do the same thing. I remember that for the first time my wife and I went to Korea, together. You know, you have to meet people you never met before, and one of the easy ways of breaking into a conversation is to say: Have you ever been in the United States? Have you ever visited the United States? And most of the people we were talking to would say: Oh, yes. Where were you? Fort Leavenworth. Right? Sure. I mean, it's a very militarized society, South Korea, as you know. If you are talking to somebody who is politically highly placed, they almost surely were military officers and ordinarily generals. That is very important in South Korea. Almost always generals, and of course, what did we do with our dependent peoples abroad? We'd bring them to the United States, Fort Bennin in Georgia. You find a lot of Central and Latin Americans at Fort Benning. And Command of General Staffs School in Leavenworth is a very important training installation and high-ranking generals abroad are very likely to have spent some time studying there. So, I mean, that's been a characteristic of imperial countries through the ages. You bring the native troops to your country, train them, and then you use them. Sure. The British promised other countries over and over again to get out of Egypt. But the precondition was that first we have to establish law and order. And once we have established law and order in Egypt we will withdraw. Well that takes decades, right? We do the same thing. The so called domino theory is very common to imperial countries who believe if you lose one thing you are going to lose another thing. It's the great game, as it's called between Britain and Russia, it is an illustration. The place in itself may not be important, but if you lose it! One loss leads to another loss and then another. Our loss is their gain. It seemed nonsensical when it was applied to Vietnam, but it is not unusual in the annals of imperialism.

Will the European Union challenge the US?
I don't think it ever will, for the reasons I gave, that is in the absence of a threat. See, Joe Parent is the guy's name, I hope he will publish the thing, or some essays from it, but he develops this … just try to think of a country to unify in the absence of an eternal threat. Well, Sweden did, but it didn't last very long and it wasn't much of a union, really. Why not? They didn't face any external threat. It's very difficult. It was one of the problems of the United States, and if you read the Federalist papers it's very well illustrated. You've got to have an external threat. Now, it was a little difficult, because the external threat was not immediate. But it was there, Britain. And it was not fanciful, I mean we did fight a war in 1812' which was not Britain's fault, it was ours. We did fight a war in 1812, they did burn the capital, Washington D.C., burned the capital building down and we fought the battle of New Orleans and all that. And you read the Federalist papers and time and time again they are making the point, again John Jay and Alexander Hamilton, the point

that if we are not united we will find ourselves split and some European countries will be dealing with Northern states and other European countries will be dealing with Southern states. And we will be the prey to the intervention of foreign powers. You have got to emphasize that external threat. You don't get internal union without external threat. Try to think of examples.

Multipolarity – will we have more wars?
The greatest guarantees of peace we've ever had, of course, are nuclear weapons. And it is difficult, almost impossible, to see how major wars can be fought by countries who have them or have the protection of those weapons. As I put it, between or among nuclear powers you can't fight in a way that enables you to gain much. Because if you are gaining much, or if it looks as though you will be gaining much, you risk retaliation. And every country knows that. You don't have to be very smart to know how much damage nuclear weapons can do. And to realize that there is nothing you can do about it, that is, the country that is raining nuclear weapons down upon you decides how much damage there will be. It is not like conventional warfare, where you can hope - and not always succeed - but you can hope to limit the damage. There is no hope. And I am bearing in mind ballistic missile defence and all that nonsense. I mean, it is just, it is impossible to imagine an effective defence against nuclear weapons because you know how small they are and how light they are. Thermonuclear - it is just not efficient - thermonuclear is about, that one to one model I looked at it in Los Alamos, it is about that long and that circumference (shows about 70 and 30 centimetres). And you can just hide that anywhere and deliver it any or a number of different means. If we had a complete 100 percent reliable ballistic missile defence we would not have a defence against nuclear weapons. It has to be just delivered the right way.

What do you think about global governance?
About what? Ah! There isn't any.

Do you think al Qaeda is a balancer to the US?
No, absolutely not. It's not capable of balancing, it is not a military power. It is not a power at all, it is not a country. Of course, it is not a balancer.

Are there new actors or actor constellations? Like in Huntington .... ?
You mean new alliance movements? Well, it doesn't make any difference, does it. Because the combined strength of the weak is not going to balance the strength of the dominant power by itself.

Is there the possibility of a neorealist foreign policy theory?
Well, foreign policy theory is very difficult. You have to figure out. You know what you are trying to explain, but you have to figure out how to do it. I don't know anybody who has written a theory of foreign policy. It's very hard to see the possibility of having a theory of foreign policy. Neorealist or whatever you wanted to call it. I am not aware of any theory of foreign policy.

What about soft-balancing? Pape?
Oh, sure. Well, you either balance or you don't. Soft-balancing isn't balancing. Right? I think what Bob Pape means is that you can see the desire of some states to balance at the same time you can see their inability to do it. And, to repeat, soft-balancing isn't balancing. How can you do soft-balancing? It's a nice term. And political scientists like to invent terms. Joe Nye is the best one in doing that. Soft power is an excellent example. Or crystal ball effect is another example. He is very good in making up terms. Bob Pape's soft-balancing is just non-balancing.

What does Neorealism say about violence?
Violence? Well, what do you expect it to say of violence? There is a lot of things theories don't say. Theories don't just say something. Well, in international politics in the realm of self-help a lot of states chose to help themselves. That is what happens. Violence is one of the possible means of trying to maintain your position in the system. That's it.

Why do you think it is appropriate not to look at the internal characteristics of the state?
Is it appropriate to look at the characteristics of states. You have to look at the characteristics of states if you try to explain what goes on in a given instance in international politics. That the characteristics of states are not in any international political theory, it is because, such a theory after all is a theory of international politics. It's not a theory of state behaviour or foreign policy, it's a theory of international politics. So, you would certainly not expect states characteristics to be in the theory. But in anybody's explanation of what in fact is going on in a given case, of course, you consider the characteristics of states.

What are the effects of unipolarity? Balancing or bandwagoning, stability or instability?
Neorealism is a theory about two or more states in international politics, it's not a theory that applies to one state. One state is not an international political theory, it is just one state. So, what you infer of course is that in the absence of a balancing state the one state is free to follow its whims, its fancies, to do as it pleases, to do what it thinks will serve it's interests, to use the position it is in. It is free to do any of those things because there is no counterbalance. What

more do you need to know? It is not a theory about one state in international politics. It is a theory about international politics. You could say that with one state - and one state only now in the world - international politics is not any longer international politics, it is the politics of the United States. You want to know a lot about what goes on in the United States, that tells you. So, you look inside the state because it is no longer really international politics. It is the politics of one state.

Why your interest in Marxist imperialism theory?

Oh, one reason I am interested in it of course is that it is an example of an inside-out theory, of course. It claims (to know) what's going on by knowing what the acting states are like. It is Wilsonian in its approach. Woodrow Wilson, Lenin, Mao Zedong, all thought in the same way that if you know what the states in the system are like, then you know what the outcomes are going to be. It's Henry Kissinger, it's Mao Zedong. They are all the same reasoning. They all reason in the same pattern. And the theory of imperialism is one of the great examples of that kind of reasoning. Schumpeter is and Lenin is, that is all the same kind of reasoning. The content is different. I mean, Schumpeter, as we well know, goes to the social factors and explains outcomes in a non-Leninist way. But in terms of content, in terms of causal direction, it is from what the states are like to the outcomes you expect. I think that is theoretically interesting and it is a very important example – theory of imperialism – is a very important example of that kind of thinking.

Do you want to explain continuity or change?

Well, both. See, that which continues is certainly not less important than that which changes. There are an awful lot of continuities in international politics. It's important to understand why you get the same things, the same patterns of action, over and over again.

Can Theory of International Politics explain the world after 9/11?

Well, before and after, yes. 9/11 did not change anything. 9/11 did not change anything. States are still the major actors, right? More so than ever before. Terrorists strengthen the state because there is only one direction people can look at for protection against terrorists and that is to the state. And states know that and take advantage of it as I said before. It enabled the Bush administration to do many of the things it wanted to do anyway.

When agents act, why is it the outcome of the system that influences the agents? Is it not the outcome of collective action?

Yeah, sure. Yes. Well, it's a system. So, the system acts on units as the units affect the system. And if you just take the sum of the actions of all the states you leave the system out. I mean that's the common way of understanding international politics. If you have good states you have good outcomes and so. That is Henry Kissinger.

You predict the rise of China already in Theory of International Politics? And: Why is there no balancing under the condition of unipolarity?

I have been concerned with China for decades, sure. Well, balancing is very difficult. It is costly, it costs money. It bears a high political cost. Why was there no balancing in the 1930ies? I mean, that is a more striking example then why there is no balancing now. As I said before, when previous great wars ended there were always enough great powers left standing to form a new balance of power. With the end of World War II, it was automatic: you had two states left, two great states left, they balance each other. All you have to know is that there are only two states. They are going to form a balance. With one state, the materials for forming a balance of power do not exist. There is no state that can balance the United States in the short term. So, it's not a question of will there be a new balance, it is a question of how long will it take! And it'll take China quite a long time even from now to be able to balance the United States. And to balance the United States it does not have to be equal in capability, but it has to be at a certain level. After all, the Soviet Union was not the equal of the United States, but it was strong enough to serve as a balancer. China has to get to that level and it is doing so, rapidly in historical terms, but when you are living through the period it seems slow. But looking back people will probably be saying: well, it only took them until the 2020ies until they were able to serve at least in a minimal way as a counterbalance to the United States.

Are asymmetrical or symmetrical structures more violence prone?

Well, asymmetric ones. It is impossible to have a major war if one power is dominant. I mean, Iraq is not a major war, it is a major annoyance. After all, winning the war in Iraq was predictably very easy. I mean, Iraq is a pip-squeak country. I mean, the problem was not defeating Iraq. That went very quickly. The problem is the problem of governance. And we have known this for centuries, as Napoleon says: you can do everything with Bayonets except sit on them. It's exactly what he is talking about. You can beat these Spaniards easily, but by god, try governing them! That's what's tough. And you don't govern them with Bayonets. Or, now, with machine guns, and mortars, and tanks, airplanes, that's not governing. So, the possibilities of resisting the conqueror are - really a conqueror's efforts to pacify the area that he's conquered militarily - are immense. And we have known this for centuries. Countries have to learn things over and over again. We are now learning what we ought to have learned long ago, but of course didn't.

What makes the security dilemma: threat or perception of threat?
Well, the dilemma is there whether you perceive it or not. If you don't perceive it you are probably going to suffer. But it isn't the perception that makes it real, it is the perception that is just the recognition that it is real. There's a lot of reality that people don't recognize, but that doesn't change the reality.

Is there room for intentions in realism?
Well, this is not what the theory is about. No.

Power strives for more power?
Oh, well, that is offensive Realism. States want to be secure and they never know how much power they need to be secure so they always need more power. Maybe descriptively true in many cases, but having too much power often proves as dangerous as not having enough. Because it scares other countries, causes them to increase their efforts or work harder to make alliances. Or both.

What about the role of ideology, norms, etc.?
We have known for a long time, that nationality, nationalism, ... in other words, the state trumps ideology. I mean, World War I is a nice illustration. The Social Democrats all around thought there couldn't be a war because the workers ... and after all, who fights the wars? By and large, the working class people. And if they are all good socialists, they refuse to fight. Ha! You think of the holy alliance. Same thing. These holy rulers were united because they were all divine right monarchs. But what triumphed in the end was not the fact that they were all divine right monarchs but that they were Germans, Russian, Austro-Hungarians and they behaved just the way you expect them to behave on national grounds, not on ideological grounds. Time and again, I mean, the idea of the revolutionary state, when Trotsky was asked what he would do, he said: I will issue revolutionary proclamations to nations that close up the foreign office. A revolutionary state does not need a foreign policy. Ha! Turned out that, of course, what the Soviet Union needed first of all was to survive. And for that you have got to have a kind of foreign policy.

Is bandwagoning or balancing to be expected?
Oh, bandwagoning is more tempting, and easier. And many states don´t have that choice of balancing or bandwagoning. They can't balance because they don't have the capability of balancing. Sure, bandwagoning is more common. Schweller for example thinks this is a refutation of balance of power theory. Well, it is not. I mean, balancing power is a strategy of survival. And every country - many countries, not every - many countries have to figure out how they can best survive. For many, the answer is: we don't have any opportunity or possibility or capability of balancing. So we better just pray and jump on somebody's bandwagon. I suspect that is what Mussolini did. Because he must have known; obviously he knew Machiavelli, obviously he knew some history, obviously he knew that when the weak ally with the strong they are going get exactly what Machiavelli told you to expect. But Mussolini did not seem to have any choices. The Italians didn't believe that the French or the British would stand up. And they had very good reasons to believe that the French and the British would not stand up. So, I think, I'd like to know the history in detail, but I suspect that Mussolini did it because he felt that he had no choice but to go with the Germans. That's an example of bandwagoning.

Can the security dilemma be overcome?
No, you can't.

What are the preconditions of peace in the future?
Nuclear weapons. Because you can't fight a war and hope to score significant gains against countries that have nuclear weapons. So, it removes any important incentives. You can have skirmishes, we know that. The Chinese and the Russians along that long Eastern border, they had skirmishes, some of that fairly sizeable. But there was never any possibility that a nuclear Russia and a nuclear China were going to fight a major war. The same thing is true with India and Pakistan. There certainly have been really major skirmishes along the line of control, but once each country had a nuclear military capability, it was clear that there was not going to be a fourth war between India and Pakistan although Scott Sagan calls the war the fourth war, because it fits the definition of more than a thousand battlefield deaths. As I say, well, there is something wrong with the definition. I don't think most Indians and most Pakistanis consider that the fourth war since independence. But it would have been a real war, I think, in the absence of nuclear weapons on both sides.

What is the effect of the North-South divide?
Well, it is bad for the South! I mean, those people who talk about globalization don't seem to know about the North-South-divide. Globalization is very much a Northern phenomenon plus Australia, New Zealand, what we think of as being Northern, industrialized, relatively rich countries. And it excludes most of the Middle East, and almost all of Africa, most of South Asia, it is just not globalization. Globalization is kind of an ideology, like interdependence. It says: Jesus, we are on the same boat. We are not. There is no globalization. There is Americanization and there is Militarization. It's not globalization. One might have thought, and I did hope, that at the end of the Cold War the military element in international politics would go down. After all, the relations between the United States and the Soviet Union were mainly military relations. They were not economic, or cultural. At least we'd ship Louis Armstrong to the Soviet Union and they would ship Ballet dancers to us. I was all for that. But that didn't amount, it was not really social interdependence, cultural interdependence, economic interdependence. The only interdependence was military. And the Cold War ended. Well, you might think that the military component would go down. It hasn't. If everything it is going up. Because the United States is free to do as it chooses and it chooses to become more and more of a militarized and militaristic state.

How would you describe the US?
Sure it is a democracy. Democracies like other forms of government make a lot of dumb choices. Not strange.

Why are more nukes better?
Oh, well, it depends. I don't know why people keep using the word proliferation. There is nothing you can do about it. I should think that everybody would know that proliferation means: spread like fire. Boom. You got one you are going to have thousands. One nuclear country, you are going to have hundreds of nuclear countries. Doesn't happen. We've had nuclear knowledge now for more than sixty years. We have nine nuclear countries. That is proliferation? No! It is not proliferation, it is the opposite. I'd say nuclear weapons spread at a glacial pace. Horizontally. Vertically, you could make an argument. After all, the United States had about 13.000 strategic nuclear weapons, and the Soviet Union had about 10.000 at their respective peaks. You could call that proliferation. But when most people use the term proliferation they mean spreading from country to country. That has never happened. And I expect it never will. But every now and then another country will get nuclear capability and that is not bad. Because every country that has acquired nuclear military capability has behaved in the same way. And one of the things about

66

nuclear weapons is very striking: is it doesn't matter who has them. See, the difference between nuclear weapons and conventional weapons, their different implications are very clear. Most people ignore them. It makes a great deal of difference with conventional weapons who has them. Right? If you get a country like Hitler's Germany, it is very difficult to contain that country, so long as there are no nuclear weapons in the world. As I wrote long ago, if Hitler had appeared in a nuclear world, it would have gone to much different results. You know, if you are going to undertake a major war, and it looks as though you are going to score major gains, you can be obliterated. And there is no ruler that comes to power in order to see his country obliterated. And one of the characteristics of dictators, authoritarian rules, fascists, whatever you want to call them, they have one characteristic in common. When we talk about rogue states, by which we don't mean the great rogue state, namely the United States, which is clearly the great rogue state in the world. We mean countries ruled by people like Gaddhafi in the old days, or Saddam Hussein, or Kim Yong Il, or before him Kim Il Sung. They have one characteristic in common: they are survivors. That means they are easy to deter. I mean, if you have a madman who would run any risk, remind as Less Aspen (n.u.) said, shortly before he became Secretary of Defence, very briefly: these countries, these rogues states are hard to deter, they maybe undeterrable. That was completely wrong. A country that is undeterrable, its rulers are not going to last long. But one of the things these guys proved to be very good of doing was discerning that line beyond which, if you go beyond that line you are going to risk your own destruction. They always had felt short of that. Until you got the worst calculator in the bunch: Saddam Hussein. And even he lasted about 25 years. Much better than even Bush the first who could not even win a second term. And Saddam Hussein pointed that out. He said: I'm here, where is George Bush? They were survivors. Now, if you are going to survive that means you have to be able to react to extreme threats to your regime. I mean, it's worth repeating: These guys are survivors, which means they are deterrable.

Do you want to influence politics with that argument?
Well, I do wish that our rulers and other rulers would appreciate that. Yes, that would be a better world if they did. And luckily with nuclear weapons even slow learners are able to survive because nobody can miss the point that if you do the egregiously wrong thing in the presence of nuclear weapons you may be obliterated. That doesn't mean you will be. But that's up to the other guy, that's up to the retaliator, and you know that.

Are you in agreement with the non-proliferation regime?
Oh, yeah, I am for it. I don't think it is very important. You see, if a country is really determined, they get nuclear weapons. Another way of saying that is if a country believes that its very survival depends on nuclear weapons it is almost impossible to prevent that country from getting nuclear weapons. I think it is much more important to get George Bush under control than it is to strengthen the nuclear regime. Well, you know, he said: three countries constitute an axis of evil, and he named them, Iraq, Iran and North Korea. And then he invades, he orders the invasion of one of them! And you're a decision maker from Iran or from North Korea, what are you going to think? There is only one way to deter the United States, and conventional weapons won't do it. That one way is by having your own nuclear weapons. Boy, I mean, I don't see how! You have a country as strong as the States and that says: I am invading your neighbour, but don't you get nuclear weapons. Oh, come on!

That is an explanation for Iran?
And North Korea.

How important is peace as a goal for international relations?
Well, international relations doesn't have and can't have any goals. Because it is not an agent, it is not an actor. The question must be: How important is peace for a given country. And that depends on many things.

You have written about the causes of war, what was that about?
Well, the causes of war lie both within particular countries and in the system. You know, it is the same old story: it is a self-help system. And countries are going to do what they think best helps them to maintain their positions in international politics. And most of the time the answer will be: maintain peace! But occasionally the answer is: go to war!. And, you know, you don't see this now, but the major powers, and now there is only one, but even if there were two or more, they had nuclear weapons that changed the game, so, you had peaceful relations. You can't fight wars to score major gains, so why fight at all? So, wars among the great and major powers have become rare. And that's a reversal, one of the many reversals produced by nuclear weapons. It used to be that you asked the question: who fights the wars? And you did not need to look it up, just say: the great powers. The great powers fought most of the wars. They suffered most of the casualties, the suffered most of the damage. And the lesser powers less so. You got nuclear weapons among the great and major powers: they can't fight. They can't fight major wars. So, there going to be wars going to be with the minor countries. Some people who read that to say:

Ok, there is less war in the centre and there is more war in the periphery. It is not necessary that there are more wars in the periphery, but they are the only wars that can be fought. Wars in the centre can't be fought.

That would also make the argument for your article 1997 "Thoughts about virtual nuclear arsenals"?
Yeah, yeah. Which I think is a lousy idea, you know.

I would like to come to your relation to international politics. Have you ever engaged in political activism?
I never marched, I never waved banners, I don't think it does much good, I've written some things. In opposition to our first war in Iraq, I did quite a bit of television-radio work in the Bay Area. Well, you know, radio stations and television stations call you up and ask you if you will appear. Sometimes if it is a radio, sometimes it is a telephone interview. But obviously not for television. And I did that for the radio, there would be several of us from Berkeley faculty and one graduate student who would appear on these programmes and talk about the first war in Iraq and the second war, our second war. I signed that petition that we talked about. I don't remember giving any talks about it, except in class. So, that's it.

Would you describe yourself as a pacifist?
Oh, no, no. I am not a pacifist. I think there are some wars that have to be fought. World War II is a good example. If I were a pacifist, strictly and honestly a pacifist, a pacifist believes that you must not fight in any war. I don't believe that. I think that there are wars that clearly have to be fought, like World War II, and wars that may have to be fought, like our war in Korea, in which I also served. I think there were some ambiguities about that one. But on balance, I don't think that was an unnecessary war, it may not have been a fully necessary war.

Which political events influenced you and in which ways?
I have not been – for the most part – a participant in politics, but a student of politics. I don't think that my political views were formed by any particular events, even major events like World War II. I didn't say: Oh, World War II, maybe I better study International Politics. Never occurred to me. I didn't study International Politics because of World War II or any other war. It developed as an academic interest without any direct influence of any particular events or experiences.

Did you ever want to influence politics yourself?
Well, I wanted to get us out of Vietnam. That's one example. I wanted to keep us out of Iraq, that's another example. Well, I'm not a political activist. Maybe I should have been, but that's not what I do. I certainly taught and did some writing against Vietnam. I wish I had done more, but that's it. I mean, I say what I think and I write what I think, but I don't go out on campaigns.

Do you think your work has some influence on politics?
Well, maybe a little over a long run. Some people in Washington tell me they read what I write and it makes them think. But I don't think that's a direct influence on anybody's policy.

Have you ever been engaged in consultancy?
Well, I was a consultant to the State Department in those heady days of interdependence where one of the papers I wrote was a State Department publication. You know, it appeared in other ways but also as a State Department thing. I went to the State Department and talked to people about interdependence. Well, I had a good audience that had just done some work on the concept of interdependence and, I don't know, I think maybe in the long run I caused some rethinking about interdependence. I mean, interdependence is a really peculiar American idea, we talked about before. And I got through to some people on that. But, I don't think that is a major influence on policy. On the nuclear front, the first paper I wrote on nuclear weapons I wrote for the CIA DoD Conference, which was then published as part of a government document. Again, some influence, but not much and not quickly and not directly. The sponsors of the conference who were surprised to find that not just me but other people took much less of an alarmist view about the existence of and the slow spread of nuclear weapons than had been expected. Now the first reaction to that document, which subsequently appeared as a Delphi paper, was horror and disbelief. But over the years people began to take it more and more seriously. That, yeah. Nuclear weapons potentially may have some bad effects. But here and now they had good effects. Certainly, nuclear weapons had something to do with the long peace. And the long peace between United States and the Soviet Union and some other countries was much preferable to a state of war among such countries. And it is not possible to believe that nuclear weapons did not have a lot to do with that. So, on the one hand, they appear to don't like nuclear weapons, which is understandable. And yet their effects have been good for all people who like peace. And I certainly do. Not everybody does, but most people do. If you like peace you ought to like nuclear weapons.

Did you ever got into trouble because of your political beliefs?
No. I mean, I taught for nine years in Swarthmorth, which is not a Quaker college, but the largest single number of people who have any kind of religious commitment have a commitment to the Quaker beliefs, including not necessarily pacifism, but a rather general pacifistic attitude. I never got in any trouble. Everybody knew what I was saying, what I was thinking, in the public debates and all that. You know.

Did you ever have to defend your political beliefs?
Sure, I mean, nuclear weapons. I mean, in many discussions, a series of discussions public, with Scott Sagan. I think they have been constructive and I think they have been one way of educating a general audience, various audiences, including audiences in New Delhi were we both happened to be at the same time, so we did one for the National Defence College, which was a good and very well informed audience. We did one for a more general audience in which I was asked a question by somebody who I was told later that this somebody was the grandson of Mahatma Gandhi. I didn't know that at the moment.

What about the end of the Cold War? Were you surprised?
Not as surprised as a lot of people. I mean, I had written that the Cold War will end and only end when the structure of international politics changes. And I was also more realistic than most people about the sharp decline in the Soviet Union, which I wrote about. Specifically in a little piece called "Another gap" but also in "Theory of International Politics" of 1979 where I said: the big question is, is the Soviet Union going to keep up? And you have to remember that that was the time when we'd be getting - in the late 1970ies and specially the 1980ies - that the people thought the Soviet Union is passing, again one of those times, the Soviet Union is passing the United States. Preposterously. Reagan when he was president said: the Soviet Union is surpassing the United States in every military category: irregular warfare, regular warfare, tactical nuclear weapons, strategic nuclear weapons, they are surpassing us in every way. No sane president ought to say something like that. But how did he end up saying it? I gave a number of talks in Asia, at the time in Indonesia and China and Japan. I would say: Wait a minute, it is not the Soviet Union who is getting ahead of the United States, it is the United States who is ahead of the Soviet Union and there is an increasing gap! And it was great fun, because they disagreed. I was able to chide. The Chinese, because there is a lot of continuity in Chinese audiences, and this was one of the [examples of] what I think of being the major institutes. You know, all the institutes are related to various establishments, for example to the military services, and this one was related to the intelligence, which in a way is the key institute, it is one of the best financed, it has an impressive

staff, it has a very impressive building, all that. And I talked to them in the early, I think it was 1982, and gave them the message that the United States was ascending and the Soviet Union was descending, which is exactly the opposite of what they believed. They believed that the Russians were coming. And, in fact, you can explain them, but the American-Russian-Chinese relations this is where perceptions were important. They changed in relations entirely in terms of those perceptions, as the Chinese saw or thought they saw the Soviet Union rising they moved toward the United States. And of course later they reversed that. And they were wrong. It wasn't the Russians who were rising, it was the Americans who were rising. And I pointed this out. Some of those people told me later - they had been in the audience the first time as well as the second - and they well remembered and I had told them and they didn't believe it.

Would you say that the world is now safer than before the end of the Cold War?
Safer for whom? It is certainly not safer for people. See, what the United States does, is not necessarily safer. For well more than a century, Latin America is an example wherever we have had dominant power we have behaved in the same arbitrary fashion in pulling force whenever we chose to. We did that at least from the late nineteenth century onward to Latin America. And now of course it is not just a hemispheric thing, it is a worldwide thing. I mean, we specialized in singling out poor and weak people and beating them up. So, if you are a poor and weak country and we don't like you, because you do something to cause us not to like you: watch out! Because we just might decide to beat you up. So you better have nuclear weapons.

Did you expect stable peace to develop after the Cold War?
Well, I expected the United States to abuse its power. That's what makes for the definition of the stable peace.

What are the dangers after the Cold War?
The dangers are the rise to dominance of one country.

Is the US an empire or a hegemon?
No, we don't have an empire in the old, traditional sense of an empire. I mean, the territorial empire, we don't have an empire in the sense in which Lenin used the term. It is more the, I call them the Neocolonialists, who say that the mere imbalance of power, imbalance of economic capabilities and whatever, varies in one way or another constitutes an imperial relation. I think, it is more an imperial relation than an empire. Or, if one prefers hegemony, I don't care which one you use: it's hegemony, it's dominance, it's severe imbalance of power, all these terms will do.

Is there a need for a new theory of International Relations?
Well, can you think of one? There you are. Nobody has thought of one. There is always a need for better theories, sure. But I don't see a particular need or possibilities there are for better theories. Someday somebody will.

What would this theory have do address?
Well, it would have to be a theory of international politics. I say politics instead of relations, because ... Again, you have to exclude some things, and relations include everything. Cultural exchanges, trade, aid, whatever, diplomacy. So, I focus on international politics. So, in getting a new theory you have to focus on international politics as the domain that you are trying to explain, that the theory is trying to explain. And I don't see any. If I saw an improved way of doing it, I would do it. I don't see the possibility. But this doesn't mean that there isn't the possibility. There's always a better theory coming along somewhere. It can come very rapidly, or it can take decades or even a century.

Let's turn to the Iraq war. Why have you been in opposition?
American government tried to make the issue of the possession or non-possession of weapons of mass destruction. And I looked at the map and you look at the balance of forces, and Iraq is a part of the world and you find that Iraq is a minor power. That is: Iran has three times the population and five times the gross domestic product and Turkey has three times the population and ten times the gross domestic product. And Israel is the major military power in the Middle East. So, you ask yourself: Saddam Hussein, even though he is a very nasty person, he has no place to go. Where is he going to go? What's he going to do to whom? Do we need to worry about him? If he has weapons of mass destruction, what is he going to do with them that could damage his neighbours, let alone damaging us? What could he do? And the answer is: he couldn't do anything without risking his own destruction. Though he proved to be so inept, or to put it more simply so dumb, that he got himself removed from the scene without even having weapons of mass destruction! But certainly, if he had had or was in the process of getting them, there was not any reason for us to think that we had to destroy them. So, Bush himself, Libby and the Bush administration were saying: Containment and deterrence no longer work. And I said: what do they mean? Do they mean that other countries can no longer deter and contain the United States? That I understand. But that we can't contain or deter other states? That is preposterous! I mean, there is a general tendency, it is not just the Bush administration, to think that although we can deter the strong, the Soviet Union especially, but also China, we can't deter the weak! Let's ask

them again. These rogue states may be undeterrable. That is nonsense! Imminently deterrable. I mean, they have been deterred. General George Bowler even thought that - and I thought this as well - in the first Iraq war, Saddam Hussein was deterred. That is when he sent the scud missiles against Israel he was careful not to arm them with highly lethal warheads. This limited the amount of the damage that they could do, some of it consequential damage, when they struck Israel - for fear of retaliation. He was deterred. And yet the same guy, General Bowler, who was Head of the Strategic Command at one time, he thought we could not deter North Korea. Why not? You can deter the strong but you cannot deter the weak? You know, it's crazy. But widely believed. Again, one of my favourites, Joe Nye, said: if nuclear weapons are going to be used, it is going to be the weak countries. The new smaller nuclear countries are going to be the first to use them. And you think: my god, how pompous can you be? I mean, this is typical of great powers: 'the great powers aren't the danger, it is the little countries. These weak little countries, they are the danger!' Oh, come on. No wonder they like Joe Nye in Washington.

What about the consequences of your position towards the Iraq war?
I was in good company. The consequences were surprisingly wide knowledge of that statement we made in the New York Times. And I think a lot of approval.

American political leaders read you. Do you think they employ you correctly, at least sometimes?
Yeah, sometimes. What do you expect? Sometimes they do, sometimes they don't. Sometimes there is no influence, the usual.

What do you agree on in American foreign policy?
Now? Very little.

What do you disagree on?
Well, I don't agree on fighting unnecessary wars. I was always against fighting unnecessary wars. I mean, that is the big thing, there are other things, but I think this is the big thing. Unilateralism in general. We are in a position where we can behave unilaterally. That doesn't mean that this is to our interest to do that or we ought to do that. It is a bit of a problem. Remember de Gaulle's famous statement when we sent somebody over to inform, we wanted to make it look like consultation, and he asked icily: Have you come to consult with me or to inform me? And it was obvious that we informed him. And even if we do in a superficial sense consult other countries, than we go ahead and do what we want to do anyway. And again, that is not an American characteristic. It's a characteristic of a dominant power.

What would you recommendations from a Realist perspective be for American foreign policy?
Well, change to the less. But that advice is not going to be taken. The only way that the United States is going to do less is that there are other countries doing more and are in a position of doing more.

What is the most important problem in international politics?
The United States.

What would be the conflicts of the future?
Oh, I think the conflicts of the future are all bound to be between the United States and China. Well, the United States is the dominant power and China will be the challenging power and the most obvious point of conflict is likely to be Taiwan. And the main-land Chinese government does not want to use force against Taiwan, but it does want to be able to yield force as an instrument for persuading the Taiwanese to do political business with China, they do a lot of economic business. And we want to deny China that opportunity to use the threat of force as a part of the bargaining with Taiwan. You know, you look at it from outside. You are not involved and I am not involved. And you think that this is something that ought to be able to figure some kind of a settlement because China does not need to exercise a direct control over Taiwan. You ought to be able to find some formula that will convince the Taiwanese to think of themselves as autonomous, not independent. And the Chinese will be thinking or believing that Taiwan is not going to try to establish it's independence. So, it will be able to smooth the thing over with euphemisms and all that. And the Chinese don't want to rule the Taiwanese, the Chinese in fact in Hong Kong, this is a good indicator, the Chinese, they always like to use numbers, as you know. Why can't it be two systems. So, the Hong Kong people have their system and we have our system, but we are all Chinese. Ok, fine. Now, if the Chinese impose themselves too heavily on Hong Kong or Macau then the Taiwanese are going to be even less willing to find any accommodation. They will say: Mind that, if we acquiesce, then we are going to be treated like the Hong Kong people are being treated. So, the main-land Chinese have to be very careful about what they do. They have to live by this 'one country, two systems'. And that could apply to Taiwan very well. And the trouble is, the Taiwanese are increasingly stubborn of course about ... they are wielding an independent country. Why is it international politics? I mean, this is probably very well domestic politics. Once you get elected, right? But from the international point of view it would be much better if they would say: Taiwanese autonomy, not independence. What's wrong with autonomy. That's what they are now. They are now autonomous. They have their

own government, they do their own thing, they go their own way. They have their own trading partners, and so on and so on. But they are not willing to do that and the mainland Chinese are not willing to say: Now you are independent. They are not willing to admit that they have a high degree of independence. And they both have their domestic political reasons, which are difficult to overcome. So, you know, I've had seminars in which I had both main-land Chinese and Taiwanese and there was a certain tension in the classroom. But they will at least superficially agree that there ought to be some way of just smoothing the situation. You don't have to be explicit about everything. It is not wise to be explicit about everything in a situation like this. Each party goes its own way really without the one claiming independence or the other claiming to be their sovereign. But will that happen? It could.

What is the most dangerous mistakes of politicians?
It's amazing how many politicians get themselves into trouble over lobbying and corruption and get caught with accepting bribes. They acquire a certain amount of power and they begin to think of themselves as being immune from anything. I mean, another governor of Connecticut, I mean, why do they do it? They get caught so often, you would think there would be a deterrent effect. It just shows you that in the absence of nuclear weapons deterrence is a very difficult thing to achieve.

A hypothetical question: If you were the president of the United States, what would you do?
Well, I would get out of Iraq. And I know this is not a good answer. People say, if we leave, there is going to be chaos. Well, I think there is chaos now. And if we withdraw hastily … How can we withdraw hastily? We have been in this thing since 2003! If we withdraw that is not withdrawing hastily, that is withdrawing very slowly. If we don't withdraw in the near future, in the next year we say, all the same arguments will apply in five years from now. And sooner or later we are going to get out. So, why not sooner? Just seems ridiculous to me. I certainly would not treat the combatants, whatever they call it, enemy combatants, the way they treat them. We have an obligation not to them but to ourselves to observe the rule of law. Habeas corpus, and other things. Whether they deserve it or not, it is an American thing, for our own self-respect. Well, you get the idea.

What should never happen again? What are the most important tragedies?
Well, I think the most important tragedy is major war.

What about 9/11. What effect did that have on you?
My wife and I were in Blue Hill at the dentists. And she was in one little room and I was in another little room, right across the hall, and the door was open. And the dentist wife had lived in Northern New Jersey and knew some people who were presumed to be in the Twin Towers because that is where they worked. So, it was directly traumatic for his wife and thus for him. And it was horrifying. When we finished with the dentist we came home, we turned the television on and we watched. It was horrifying. Sure, of course it was.

How would you explain to yourself why this has happened?
Well, there is nothing unusual about terrorists. They have been there for centuries. The thugs, it goes way back into biblical times and medieval times in various parts of the world. There is nothing new about terrorism. With the advance of technology of course, terrorists can act in ways that are more spectacular. And, although I think that terrorism generally is being inefficient, there is a lot of evidence that terrorists are pretty … like this guy in the airplane trying to inflame his shoes with a kitchen match. Come on! Or the terrorists who have been recently caught in London, and of course the British are very good at dealing with terrorists, because they have all this experience from dealing with the Irish. And they are very good at it. And the terrorists ought to know that. One of these were caught parking in a no-parking zone. I mean, a lot of these terrorists are laughable. But this one was obviously very well planned. And it wasn't the terrorists who were inefficient. It was the American authorities who were inefficient. And they were able to pull off a spectacular terrorist attack.

What do you think are the reasons for this attack?
In a bipolar world, the weak and the disadvantaged could hope to play off one country against another. They can't do that anymore. They have to deal with the United States, period. The dominant power is always a major target. And of course, since we are a major presence, even aside the war in Iraq we are a major presence in the Middle East, our longstanding highly biased support for Israel and favouring Israel over the Palestinians, which we have obviously done over and over and over again over a long period of time, and the stationing of American troops in Saudi Arabia and all that naturally arouses the ire of certain Muslims and the object of their ire has to be the United States. To a lesser extent Britain because of its old and longstanding commitments in the Middle East. But in terms of major actions in the Middle East now, it is the United States that makes itself a major target. And if you do that you have to expect the consequences.

So, what is to be done about it?

You can't do much. I mean, we are doing various things not necessarily doing them very well, airport inspections and all that. But in the end, if you have a determined and skilful leader of terrorists, they are going to be able to do something pretty damaging. And, you know, what most people are very concerned about - weapons of mass destruction especially, nuclear materials not necessarily, nuclear bombs - now what can you say? It's possible. It is difficult for terrorists to handle weapons of mass destruction, whether chemical or biological and especially if they are nuclear, but it is possible, and all you can do is you do your best. And all you can say is that, well, if you are talking about countries and there is a nuclear attack, countries can sustain military activity, terrorists cannot. So, there is a self-limiting quality to terrorist actions. But that self-limiting quality does not exclude the possibility of them using nuclear materials in ways that would be highly damaging but localized geographically and limited to in an extent by the fact that they can't keep repeating those actions.

Some reflections. What would you do if you could start another life?

I'm happy with it. As I say, I wanted to get back into the political philosophy game. But I don't any longer. I find International Relations a very convenient object of study.

So, you would again choose academia?

Yes, I definitely would.

Can the gaps between the debates be bridged?

Well, let's hope not. I mean, no debates no fun, and no progress either. I mean, if we don't have disagreements, we have stasis.

What are the main problems in IR to be solved currently?

The main problem is always war and peace, that's the main problem. It's not trade, aid, more important ... the main problems are always how to maintain peace how to prevent war!

Is IR developing in the right direction?

I don't see it developing at all. I don't. You know, if you read the journals, I don't see the development.

What would you tell the IR community, what has to be done?
Just the usual. We are not going to change the IR enterprise very much, not in the short time, certainly. I think we are going to read by and large the very same dull and dreary stuff for some years to come.

(The following excerpts are from interviews half a year later with Kenneth Waltz in New York.)

You asked me what my failures were, and I never answered that question.

Can you answer that now?
Sure. Acting, for years. When I was in eighth grade - that would be about the age of 13 - I was scrooge, in "A Christmas Carol". And I thought "I must be pretty good at acting, because it's the lead part". And, for some years thereafter, when somebody would say: What do you want to be? I'd say: I want to be an actor. I had various parts along the way; and I didn't realize that the reason I got these parts when I was young is because I could memorize the lines, I could stand on a stage and face the audience, and I could speak loud enough for them to hear me. So I began to think "You know? Maybe I could be an actor". As I got older, I kept at it, and I kept getting worse and worse parts. And I didn't really catch on, until I was in college, that I was just no good at it. I should've awakened earlier to my lack of acting ability; but it took a while, quite a while.

What I would like to start with is the question of nuclear weapons. I would like first to ask you to try broadly to explain what you'd tell us about nuclear weapons and nuclear peace. What do you say?
Well, let me tell you how I got in to the nuclear business. I had finished "Foreign Policy and Democratic Politics" - no, I'd finished "Theory of International Politics". It was now published; it was in press. And so I was kind of free. And I had a phone call from a fellow at the C.I.A., who was planning, with the Department of Defence, a conference on nuclear weapons. And, since I didn't have a commitment, and since I had been thinking that I really had not spent enough time - I hadn't really thought, seriously and deeply, about the implications of nuclear weapons - and, of course, in teaching national security policy, I covered that subject, but I hadn't done it really in depth. So I said yes. And I wrote a paper. And the conference was a good conference. Dick Betz was at it; Bob Jervis was at it, and a number of other people. It was really an unusually good conference. And, later, the paper that I wrote became the Adelphi paper, which you know about. And I concluded, in thinking about this, and in relating it to what I had been teaching and discussions with some of my students, that nuclear weapons were really good weapons for

keeping the peace. In other words: I agreed with Bernard Brody, who, I think is the most remarkable person in the nuclear field. 1946, I mean he must have written his essays in 45, must have written them right after the bombs were dropped. He really foresaw the future, the world as affected by nuclear weapons. So, I developed that, and published the Adelphi Paper and some subsequent reflections on nuclear weapons.

So, what is your main argument?
The main argument is that nuclear weapons are the greatest peacekeeping weapons the world has ever known.

Why do you say so?
Because anybody who is sane and has a moderate amount of intelligence realizes how much damage nuclear weapons can do. The decision about how much damage to do rests not with the person who will receive the damage, but the country that will inflict it. This means that anybody who tries to achieve significant gains militarily against a nuclear country knows and can't avoid knowing that it may suffer catastrophically. Now, this of course came to be known as Mutual Assured Destruction, which is a completely misleading term, because you don't need to destroy a country in order to deter it. You just need to be able to or appear to be able to inflict a high degree of damage. It doesn't really make any difference whether or not you can do that, as long as the other country believes that you may be able to do it. So, deterrence is both very effective and very easy to achieve. What is very striking about this is that - one of the many striking things about nuclear deterrence - is that every country who has acquired nuclear weapons has behaved in the same way. That is, it does not make any difference whether nuclear weapons are possessed by a moderate democratic country, such as we used to be, or whether a country such as George Bush has turned us into or whether the country ruled by Adolph Hitler. Nuclear weapons affect the behaviour, both of the possessor of the weapons and the possible victims of that country.

So, would you say that for this deterrent effect, the Cuban missile crisis for example or the...
Yeah, that's one of my favourite examples. I remember, my reflection is that I was teaching at Swarthmore. Some of my students who I was teaching then have reminded me that when the crisis occurred, I said: Don't worry. Nuclear weapons are involved; nobody is going to use them. For the reasons I just gave. We had naval superiority in local waters; we had nuclear weapons, nothing to worry about.

OK. What do you think in this light about - I mean, there was some talk about using nuclear weapons by the United States as well as by France or Iran recently.

See, there is always talk about using nuclear weapons. There was talk about using nuclear weapons in our Korean War. There was talk about using nuclear weapons in Vietnam and the China war. I mean, there is always talk about it, that doesn't mean anybody is going to do it. Military and political leaders are supposed to consider all the possibilities. Their weapons are one of the possibilities, but it would be strange if the question didn't come up, but the answer has always been the same: Don't.

But in the case when the other country, which is targeted, doesn't have nuclear weapons. The rationale changes. For example, Iran is targeted, but Iran does not have nuclear weapons. We can actually target it with nuclear weapons because they cannot retaliate. Is that right?

They cannot retaliate with nuclear weapons, but that doesn't mean they're impotent. It would have been very costly for us to use nuclear weapons in Iran, which apparently we ultimately realized. There are many things Iran could have done. And also in many cases in which the country doesn't have nuclear weapons, it has other countries who are directly interested, who may or may not be allies but are directly interested, who have nuclear weapons. It's a frightening prospect just to contemplate the use of nuclear weapons. Even against a country who doesn't have any. Well, when the strong face the weak, the strong country with nuclear weapons doesn't need to use them. We don't need to use nuclear weapons against Iran even if we wanted to inflict severe damage of Iran. We could perfectly well do that conventionally. And when you come right down to making a decision, then the question arises, you know, why would you want to ... it's, it's a more specific question. The general question is: Why would you want to go to war against a weak country? The answer is that countries do that often to their ultimate dismay. As now with the United States and Iraq. Or earlier with the United States and Vietnam. I mean, obviously we were strong and Vietnam was weak, and obviously we are strong and Iraq is weak. But the weak can extract considerable costs from the strong. They can't win. And I opposed the war in Vietnam long before it started. In fact, specifically beginning in 1963. For two reasons. One was a general and a natural political reason: it didn't matter who won. As Henry Kissinger ultimately said, it took him a long time, Brezhnev said about who wins and who loses: It doesn't affect the world balance of power. Well, that was easy to know in advance! And the other thing is I had read a lot of Meradigon and I was well aware of the costs that guerrillas or irregular warfare can extract from powerful countries. I mean, there is the history of the Ballihaps in the Philippines. There is the history of terrorism in Malaya, as it then was. I mean, the British prevailed but at tremendous costs. Why would you want to fight over an area that is irrelevant in terms of the balance of power between two major countries, when the expected costs are immense? The chances of success are low.

Nowadays I would say that the situation is different. And I would say that nowadays the United States is trying to establish their own world order, their own system of international relations. And therefore the incentive to win is just to establish their own power structure in certain regions that are opposed to this power structure.

Yeah, in fact this goes back to the memorandum of 1946, and it was supplied through Harry Truman, President Truman, by Clark Clifford in which he said the struggle is a struggle for world order. It's not a struggle for this or that piece of territory but for world order. And of course, very powerful countries, and especially countries that may be world-dominant, I mean, they take that as their mission. Now the question is: Should they? I mean, is that a sensible idea? Is that in the national interest of that country? And that answer is usually: No, it isn't. Because we know what aspiring world-dominant countries have come to from ... Where do you want to start? Louis the XIV. You can go way back. I mean, that's Alcebiades vs Inicious. And Inicious, the wise old general said: Don't! Don't! Stop! Stop! Overextending and all that. And Alcebiades, the fiery orator. Syracuse, all that. Over and over again. Countries don't learn.

Let's return to the nuclear issue. What do you think about the danger, which is cited very often today, that terrorists use nuclear weapons?

I think that is a greatly exaggerated worry. In the first place, the dangers that terrorists pose are greatly exaggerated. There are political scientists such as Joe Nye who say that terrorists can now operate at a level comparable to those of middle powers of the world. Well, that's absolute nonsense. They can't! I mean, they can't sustain a military operation; they can't occupy and administer territory. They can't threaten the fabric of a society. They can do what terrorists have done through the ages: strike in ways that are locally damaging and highly annoying. As for example, the twin towers. I mean, almost 3.000 people killed. You know, that's significant. It's not a minor act, but it's hardly comparable to one country attacking another country. We just get carried away with these things. Now, a nuclear ... most terrorists don't want nuclear weapons. I mean, they're a pain in the neck. You have to enlarge the terrorist group because you've got to acquire them. Even if you steal them, or buy them or something like that. And who are you going to steal them from? And who are you going to buy them from? You know, if you had nuclear weapons, would you want to sell them to terrorists? That's the last thing in the world that you'd want to do because terrorists can't do you much ... they can't help you much. Right? Maybe they can make a payment. But they can't help you in your future relations with other countries. They can only hurt you. And after all, you may be found out. And a country like the United States, bumbling though we are, has tremendous abilities to find out what other countries are doing. In all kinds of ways. So, you know damn well if you do it, you might be found out. You can't, see ... now here's the thing. You can't help but know that. You don't have to be very smart. But just know you might be found out. And then there's the further thing. For example, if somehow a nuclear weapon had been used when Saddam Hussein was ruler of Iraq - even if we didn't know where the hell the thing came from – we'd say: Saddam! Hang on Saddam! And I'd hope we wouldn't use nuclear weapons against him. But we would've done something very damaging. You don't want to fool around with nuclear weapons. Terrorists or not terrorists. We used to say the Soviet Union was always threatening us with nuclear weapons. You know, you go back and look at the record. We were threatening the use of nuclear weapons against the Soviet Union at least as much as they were threatening us. So, sure people talk that way. Osama Bin Laden talks that way. Does that mean he wants to have them and would use them? Not necessarily. And one person doesn't decide to use them. I mean, there were some very nice satirical pieces where the ruler says: Drop a nuclear weapon on New York City. And the person who's receiving the commands says: What? What am I supposed to do? How do I do that? Who's going to help me? I mean it takes a whole bunch of people to do this sort of thing. I mean, the worry's not zero. But the door, I think, is very small. And there's a further thing, it's self-limiting. Terrorists can acquire a nuclear warhead; they drop it, that's probably the end of them. And people tell me: Well, yeah, but they don't care because they get to go to heaven and all that. But, I don't notice that the leaders of these terrorist organizations reason that way. They seem to be very good at getting their followers, the zealots, to reason that way and commit suicide bombing and all that.

My final question to nuclear weapons; what about the American missile shield? Will that in any way change the equation?
This is such a boon-doggle. Ever since this question of defending against nuclear weapons has come up - and it goes way back to at least President Nixon, and it goes back farther than that, in fact – it's been said, rightly, that the cost-benefit analysis always favours the offence. Any number of people has said this. Casper Weinberger when he was Secretary of Defence, Khrushchev, McNamara. I mean, if they erect defences, we'll increase the number of our offensive weapons. And the offence always wins because in the case of nuclear weapons the offence is always much cheaper than the defence. So, it's what we call a mugs game. In other words, you're a fool to play it. You're a fool to play the defensive game. We do it, but to a minor extent. It's so easy to overwhelm the defense. And in fact, nuclear defense is not only hopeless but they are counterproductive because what they do is encourage the potential adversary to add to his

offensive capabilities. Attacks are going to fail anyway. And then to somebody like Friedman Diceman - who is well known for saying a number of not dreary, terrible things – said: Well, but, nuclear defences are very good for the cities they do defend. Now, if you were living in a city that's a potential target, wouldn't you like to have nuclear defences? No! The answer is no. Moscow had nuclear defences, right? What did we do? Exactly what you would expect us to do. We targeted Moscow with a larger number of missiles and warheads. So, defences aren't going to work very well. You're just going to be destroyed six times instead of two times. Right? You're just going to target as many offensive warheads as you think you need to take the defences out. And that's military. All countries reason this way. I mean, if you think you need, lets say ten warheads to do it, well you better be safe make it 20. Right? If you're living in a country - a potential target - if you're sensible you would say: Please don't build nuclear defences in our city! And it's odd because when one of the times - and this became a big subject of controversy in the United States - one of the worries was that if we decided to defend, say, Boston - this is real case because we decided to defend Boston - the initial worry was that people in Detroit would say: Why Boston? Why not us? Is Boston better? You don't care if we get destroyed, you only care about Boston? Exactly the opposite happened. People didn't want these damn defences in their own backyards so to speak.

The first question is if you have to summarize your theory to an ignorant person - a person that does not know about your theory - how would you do that?
Well, like that guy put it pretty succinctly, in the book. The first chapter, which is a brief chapter all about theory, which I think, at least at the time was a unique chapter because people never said - they used the word theory. Still do. You hear it all the time; it's a very political science department at Columbia. Some of the students point this out to me; almost nobody says what he means by the word theory. When I set out to write theory of international policies, the first thing I have to do is figure out what I mean and what I think it should mean by the word theory. And I am not told by some philosophers of science that. Philosophers of science people are pretty well coming around to the view that I stated in that first chapter with the distinction between laws and theories, and hypothesis and laws and all, and theories at the end. So the theory has to explain the law. You can't find laws and regularities of behaviour, in the case of political science. If you don't have those regularities of behaviour that is repeated over time and under a variety of conditions, then there's no possibility of that in theory. I took balancing as being the recurrent behaviour. And then the theory explains those recurrent behaviours in terms of the interests and basics. You assume basic motivation, which is to survive, and you look to condition two or more countries coexisting in a world of self-help. They each tend to their own security and this leads to internal

efforts to become stronger and external efforts to make alliances where they are needed or useful. That's it.

Another question on "Theory of International Politics": Is there, and what do you think is the most common misperception of the theory, if there is one?
Well, I'm sure there is one. It drives me nuts. Pushed by an ordinary mosquito might be the best example. People who say I ignore internal politics. A theory has to be about something, as I say over and over again. And this one is about international politics. It's not about domestic politics. But to draw the inference that because it's a theory of international politics one believes or assumes that internal politics are unimportant is simply a profound misunderstanding of theory. Of course internal politics, I wrote a book about it. Of course different states behave differently. And of course that's important, internal politics. But now, that's one thing. The theory of international politics is another thing. Now put the two things together. Economists do this all the time. And since I began life as an economist, professionally, this struck me as being no problem. Economists do this all the time. There's the behaviour of the foreigner on the one hand and the behaviour of the American on the other hand. The two are distinct but related. I said this often through international politics. People are going to get tired of reading this because I repeat it. It didn't do any good.

Let's turn to something else. I would like to ask you a little bit about other scholars. First about Bob Keohane. Can you tell me again how you met him, what you think about him?
Sure, sure. When I was at Swarthmore we wanted to hire somebody in the international field. I can't remember who else we interviewed, but I can remember very well when we looked at Bob Keohane's usual transcripts, and recommendations. When we interviewed him, we concluded immediately and unanimously we want to hire this guy. Very impressive on paper and very impressive in person. That was my introduction to Bob Keohane, and he and I were on the faculty together at Swarthmore for, I can't remember exactly how long, but a for couple of years, anyway. Not only were we colleagues, but we became good friends, and we've been good friends ever since. I'm sure in his view as well as my view. I think he's really a good person. He's very bright, he works very hard, he's a good teacher. He's got all of the characteristics you would want in a colleague. I don't see a lot of him anymore, but every once in a while we have long phone conversations. He's basically a structural realist, as he says. As he and Joe say in one or more other pieces, that their approach, their institutional theory is built on structural realism. I can't find any theory, institutional theory, that goes beyond structural realism. There's a concern, obviously, that's different from that of most structural realists, and that is a concern for

institutions and what they do. As Keohane says, when the chips are down, and it's an important matter of security, well, structural realism prevails. He's not at all shy about saying that, writing that.

Actually, I spoke to Bob Keohane, and he said the same thing that you said about him, of yourself, that you are brave, dedicated, hardworking and a very good teacher. He said that everyone who is seriously doing good theories is also a good teacher.
I'm not sure that everybody who is doing good theory is a good teacher, but I hope that's right.

Is there any experience or event, which describes your relationship between you and Bob Keohane best, like a significant event or experience together?
Well, I don't think there was any one thing. We went back to the beginnings long ago, and we were on the faculty together. We have been on panels together of course at the American Political Science Association over the years. All the exchanges have always been stimulating and I think constructive. I think we have had a very good interaction.

Let me turn to Justin Rosenberg, because I know you know him from LSE. How did you get to know him and how did you interact?
Well, in the old days - well, let me start again. Over the decades, my wife and I have lived in London for about four years. The first time beginning in 1959, and I was working on what ultimately became foreign policy and democratic politics. So, I was not attached to, but I began to spend time at the London School of Economics. I liked it, and my wife liked it very much indeed. In fact our two favourite universities are Columbia and the LSE. The LSE in those days had an outstanding international relations department, a separate politics department. Charles Manning was the professor. In those days, there was just one professor per department, and Hedley Bull and Martin Wight were in my view the outstanding members of that rather large international relations department. We got to know them and their families very well indeed. I also of course was working in the politics department, not just the international relations department, because of my just comparing politics with foreign policy in the two countries. There were good people like – what's the guy who died prematurely, Bob, he was a Canadian, wrote the big book on Labor Party Politics. Damn, I like Bob, he did a lot of - he was prominent on radio and television and a lot of interviewing. He happened to be on leave the year we were there but we got to know him, we got to know him very well. He had established a seminar that was well known and highly regarded, invited political people, cabinet ministers and MPs and party officials and labor union officials. That was carried on by a couple of - in his absence - a couple of other

86

faculty members. I went to that seminar; Bernard Crick was one of the people. So, I got to know him. Then of course, I interviewed a lot of political people of all sorts. So, I really got involved deeply in British politics, but it really began through the LSE. So I think I knew just about everybody in the politics department and in the international relations department. And some of them we got to know better than others. Ken Minogue. I don't know if you know of him. Bernard Crick. Bob, whatever his last name is. And of course, best of all, Hedley Bull and Martin Wight. We still see their wives, but they've unfortunately both been dead for some time. Not their wives, the husbands have been dead for some time, which is a shame. We had a great time, both the political people... We had a farewell party that we gave at our flat. Two MPs came, neither of whom we had invited.

Let's return to Justin Rosenberg. He was there at LSE...

I doubt he was there then. He's not that old. That would be subsequent to '59 and '60. So I began in '59, '60, because that was the beginning, and then every time we went back to live in the London thereafter, I was connected in one way or another. I spent one year in the philosophy department, '76 to '77, because that's when I was working on "Theory of International Politics". And as you probably know, the philosophy department teaches philosophy of science, period. That's all they do. Start with Kant, which is the right place to start, and at least last time I was there, that's the only traditional philosopher that they really devoted a course to. The rest of it was all theory, theory, theory so to speak. And they did it at a very high level. It was very good. I really liked that. Then the next time I went back, I was in the international relations department. So, I knew most everybody in the department over a period of years. Last time we were there, I think it was '91, '92. I could be a year off.

Let us turn to, because you mentioned it before and because you have the interview here. So I would like to ask you, are you aware of Alexander Wendt's work? Because in his work, in his book on constructivism, he actually says in this interview, he says he wrote this book in order to rewrite your book, "Theory of International Politics". What do you think about this?

I think there's a lot in that. In fact, I think it was 1991, 92. We had occasionally been of correspondence. I remember this because I was in London, living in Ken Minogue's flat, as a matter of fact, near Swiss Cottage. Nice flat. And he said in one of his letters, sometimes his students at Yale say, "What is it you that really disagree about with Waltz?". And I think there's less distance between us than many students believe. Now, in a way everybody's a constructivist. You can't say anything without constructing something. You're not reflecting reality; you're reflecting on reality. But I'm not a constructivist, as you know, in the sense in which the trend has

87

come to be in the social sciences; and he considers himself to be a constructivist. So, when he writes, as he has written, a length piece on the inevitability of the world state. I disagree with that completely: I don't think there's even a possibility of a world state, let alone an inevitability. So, yes, we have disagreements. But I do respect his work. I assign parts of his book; I've read it carefully; I think it's a very intelligent book. I think he's the best thing, by far, in the constructivist vein; I don't think there's any competition for it. But, in the end, we have our differences.

How would you describe the main difference between you? He's just said you're actually very close. So what is the main difference?
Well, the main difference is that he thinks that people can choose - how does he put it? His "self-interest" and "other-regarding". Well, you know, you can't. And, you know, it goes back to my basic view that, in so far as you are living in a self-help world, you have be self-regarding, or suffer. Or risk suffering: you don't always suffer; sometimes, you're lucky. But you have to behave in a self-regarding fashion, or risk losing, suffering, whatever. And it's true in the business world; it's true in international politics; it's true, in so far as there's a world of self-help. And, obviously, the extreme example of that is international politics. There are many examples inside of states; but there are limits inside of states that exist because of civil society and government.

And this self-help, or self-regarding, is due to the institution of anarchy.
Well, if you want to call it an institution - yeah, you can call it an institution, yeah. The anarchy corridor, yeah. And, as I was saying, that's why it applies, in part, inside of states: because many parts, many segments of society, are basically self-regarding. Competitive economy is a good example. But that's limited as compared to international policy: it's limited by governmental rules and interventions and so on.

So how would you then regard the role of international institutions?
Well, they're major if they serve the interests of the most- or the more-powerful countries. I mean institutions: sovereignty, for example. All you have to do is read Steve Krasner: he's very good at this. Or institutions generally: I mean they are designed, and used, by major countries to serve their interests. And, now, I know that institutionalists go in and get, as an example - say that "Yes; but, over time, institutions come to be accepted and begin to have an effect on –". Only so far, and so long, as the more-powerful states find that the institutions serve their interests. The cluster of institutions that we refer to when we say Bretton Woods, when we found that they no longer, we believe that they no longer served in the interest of the United States, that makes some shocks. Shocks is a good word there, because a lot of people, a lot of other countries, a lot of

officials in other countries, were really surprised, they effectively said "Hey, we don't like these institutions anymore, we are going to change them; we are going to change them".

OK, last question regarding other scholars: Can you tell me a little bit about those people which have been influenced by you, which you could maybe call your students or your followers? Like I think of Mearsheimer, maybe Gilpin, Snyder and so forth. How do you know them, how do you relate to them, have they directly learned from you, have you interacted with them?

Well, Gilpin, I didn't really get to know him until quite late in our respective careers, by quite late, certainly not until the 1980's. God, I think I have it right, I may have met him through a classmate or something, but I don't think I really got to know him until the 1980's, by which time we were both pretty well on our careers. Snyder, goes way back to, in fact I can say specifically, I was a research assistant for Bill Fox, and his father died unexpectedly. Got a phone call from his secretary saying: "Professor Fox is going to Chicago, and he'd like to have me take his graduate seminar", which was to meet the next day. So, we did, and Ben Snyder was in that seminar, and came to see me subsequently because he was interested in what we were talking about, with Bill, and I've known him well ever since. I was, I guess, a little ahead of him in the graduate program, we were in the same program, and approximately in the same phase of that program, so we got to know him and his wife, and subsequently his children. I guess it was his wife's father, who was a good ukulele player as well. So that's Gilpin, who else did you ask about? Mearsheimer. Oh, again, that came later. He, and probably not even before this, he was one of the people asked by the Council on Foreign Relations to write a book on their usual council way; that is to surround the potential book writer with a group of scholars of varied interests, and then the potential book writer writes a chapter. When he's got a chapter ready, have a meeting to discuss the chapter. I think that's the first time I actually got to know him anyway; he and my wife and I had supper together on occasions and all that, so I got to know him pretty well. Yeah, I liked him, and I admire him greatly as a scholar. As a speaker, he's got real force, intellectual force.

Let us run to some questions about friends and family. What would you say - I assume you have been a very work-centered person. But what role, for you, personally, do your friends and your family play in your life?

Family plays a tremendous role. We've been married 58 years. And I was a graduate student at Columbia when I met my wife, who was then working in the treasurer's department at AT&T. And she was working for two reasons: one, because she wanted to save money to go to Europe; and, the other, because she wanted to save money to go to graduate school. And, after we got married - see, we met in '48, late spring; and we got married in '49. And she worked that summer; and then she quit and went to graduate school, in the same department. And, when I met her, I was a graduate student in economics. And so she went through this whole tormented period in my life, where I had come to realize I was not going to be an economist and didn't know exactly what I would be; and so she lived through that, which was difficult. And then we went to graduate school together. And she and I were both in political, not international politics. So we did all that together. And then, when I was called back into the Army and went to Korea, she did all the work for one of the chapters in what became the book, my first book: the behavioural science chapter, about which she was heroic, because she read all that junk. And I would get plenty of letters in Korea, saying "Can't I stop? You want me to read still more of this idioticness?" And my answer was always "No! This is just what I want!" So she did all the work on that chapter, and a lot of work subsequent to that on my work. And the family, the kids, were - there were three boys; two survived. And the one in Alaska was a tremendous reader: he reads more than anybody, even more than Robert Jervis, who is like the biggest reader that I know. He sends me books to read; and he's very good. The younger boy is a lawyer, but international law, so it's not unrelated. We see a fair amount of each other.

What does the son in Alaska do?
Drives a taxi. Why? I don't know. What he likes to do is read. Nome, Alaska, is not much of a town; it's certainly not a city: So he has a lot of time, so he can kill a lot of free time. And he's just been there for decades. I don't know why. But he just doesn't – there's nothing there: very few people.

So did you try to influence your kids in a certain way? Did you expect them - or try to - follow you in your path?
I was astonished when our first born went to college, first went to Oberlin. Which is where my wife and I went. And that's the last thing we expected, that he would follow in our footsteps so-to-speak. And he divided his college career about evenly between Berkeley - when I was in the faculty there - and Oberlin, getting his first degree at Berkeley. Then he became a graduate student in politics at Berkeley. In fact was in his undergraduate he took a course around from me, but it was about 100 students. Understood so the students still making of a teaching assistant and does the grading and everything. And as a graduate student he didn't take a course or seminar from me. But he came to the seminar and didn't miss a session. And since he and I, as fathers and sons do have - when the kids are in their teenage years - we had our troubles and our conflicts. And then I was relieved, surprised, and of course gratified, that he would choose to do that. And now we get along very well as is true for the rest of the younger one, who went to Santa Cruz-University of California. When he was in high school he used to come to one of my lecture classes and in fact he would bring his friends, often young ladies, high school students.

90

And then he would pretend to be a student at Berkeley. And he'd say, after class he'd talk to the other students. He'd say: "Is this guy any good? I'm thinking about taking his course next year. What do you think of it?" Does international commercial law. But now does a lot with oil and stuff.

Can you describe what attracted you to your wife? What was the attraction about?
Well she was a very attractive person and seemed to be very bright, intelligent person. There were four girls living together in an apartment at that time. It's also true now, it was very difficult to find apartments in New York City, it was 1948-49. And it wasn't just a question of money; it was a question of just finding any kind of apartment. You couldn't even get a telephone. She didn't have a telephone even though she worked in the treasurer's office at AT&T. So she could use a telephone at will when she was at work but those girls couldn't get a telephone in their apartment. And this is not just right after the war! This is 1948. It's kind of a surprise. But I could call her at work and get my nickel back because it was American Telephone and Telegraph; so you just dialled the number, ask for her, and the nickel would come right back. That was nice. And she could call anywhere in the world without any payment. So if I was back at Ann Arbor, whatever, she could call me. It was nice. But that's not what attracted me that was all just subsequent. But I thought she was nice looking, I thought she was very bright, bright mind and all that. So we got together and that's sort of what happens.

First question, was there ever a crisis in your life?
Oh yeah, there was a crisis about what the devil am I going to do? I'm not going to do - I mean the first thing was really in high school. I mentioned before that I had just grown up thinking I was going to go to the University of Michigan to become an engineer. Then I began to realize I wasn't going to become an engineer because I wasn't interested in engineering. About - as I recall - about 24 hours of sessions at the University of Michigan, when I was in high school, about career counselling. And I realize in retrospect that I must've been dealing with graduate students in psychology or something like that. When it was all done and I was ready for the evaluation a woman said to me, "Your greatest ability's in music".

Kind of difficult. Is there anything that generally brings you pleasure?
I love music. Well, I'd say my favourite composers are Bach. I don't know if were - there is a Columbia college radio station and they play, whole of week around from Christmas to New Year's. It's fairy tales, and I'm very fond of Berlios. We liked a good deal of modern, even contemporary music as well. We don't do it so much anymore, but we used to go to the chamber

music in the summer, which is very good. They have wonderful faculty concerts. Sherry Grossman (sp), first cellist at the Metropolitan Opera Orchestra is their regular cellist. They have others, also well known, but he's the principle one that comes every summer. Very well-known people on the faculty. There's a violinist from the Julliard quartet. Marian Han from the Oberlin Conservatory, was Oberlin Conservatory, she's a pianist. She's very good. They just have wonderful musicians. They run a summer school for young instrumentalists who give their own concerts. It's very high level stuff and we used to go to every one of those. But it's getting difficult for my wife to do that, so, we don't go as much anymore. But they also broadcast those events subsequently recorded the broadcast. We listen to classical music almost all the time.

What would an ideal day look like for you?
I get up I read the New York Times at breakfast and after. I turn the classical music on right away and I spend a lot of time reading. That's what I do mainly. Of course, I used to teach more than I teach now. I've always enjoyed teaching, some grading exams and all that. I've always enjoyed the teaching part of it. Still do. We like to go to operas and plays. We like to go out to eat. Oh, I used to love to play tennis. I wish I still could, I obviously can't. You have to be able to move. We used to play a lot of tennis, especially at … Well, of course, before, but especially at Berkeley. We had quite a tennis playing department, graduate students and faculty. I usually played with younger people. I was not a great player. But, for a person who is not a natural born athlete I did pretty well. Took lessons. I took one lesson a week, and lessons are more strenuous than playing because the instructor after a while began to use a machine and the machine is relentless. You hit a ball and there's another ball. I think it's a great game. It only takes two … you can do it by yourself against the backboard, but really to play you have to have two people, at least.

Coming to the next question, is there anything important which you would say "This is what I have learned in the course of my life, this is my lesson I have learned this," any wisdom that you have come to?
I put a high value on reading and thinking. I think I like the same basic things such as reading and thinking. To me that is the basis. I mean you read and you think. By reading I don't mean just doing research. I mean reading literature. I mean, for example, when I was writing a book that was partly about British politics, I read an awful lot of drama and these Railing's novels, George Elliot. That was great stuff.

Do you think you have reached your goals in life to the full extent? Or is there anything that you....
Goals sort of develop in the process of the life. When we were graduate students we thought well we'll end up in some relatively obscure liberal arts college. I was kind of surprised when that didn't happen. It's worth more than that relatively obscure liberal arts college and then, of course, we went on from there. I've never had governmental ambitions, or political ambitions.

What would you say is your greatest achievement in life?
Well, I think Theory of International Politics says it.